# Mastering

# Pension Wealth

## A Step-by-Step Guide

### Including In-Depth Analysis and Strategies To Defeat Online Fraud

**Yemmi Agbebi MBA**

**How I Became A Pension Millionaire On A Salary By Earning More, Saving More and Starting Early - A Planning Guidebook With Proven, Practical Templates and Tips**

First published in the United Kingdom in 2025

By Alexa Bratski Publishing

An imprint of Alexa Bratski Publishing

Contact details: alexabratski.publishing@vondalust.com

This edition First published in the UK in 2025

by Alexa Bratski Publishing

Printed, bound and distributed by IngramSpark

| Cover Design by Olayemi Bolaji

A catalogue record for this book is available from the British Library.

eBook: ISBN 978-1-0682483-0-6

Paperback: ISBN 978-1-0682483-1-3

Hardback: ISBN 978-1-0682483-2-0



The information given in this book should not be treated as a substitute for professional financial advice; always consult a certified and FCA regulated financial adviser. Any use of information in this book is at the reader's discretion and risk. Neither the author nor the publisher can be held responsible for any loss, claim or damage arising out of the use, or misuse, of the suggestions made, the failure to take financial advice.

Reader Discretion Advised: Users are encouraged to exercise caution and discretion when visiting external or third party websites, as these sites are outside the control of the author and publisher.



Owned by Alexa Bratski Publishing 2025

alexabratski.publishing@vondalust.com

"Everything I have ever done in my life—every decision, every sacrifice—was, in its own way, preparation for what lay ahead. It all led me to this point: wealth in retirement or mere existence". I decided there and then that I would enter retirement not diminished, not haunted by the regret of failing to plan, but enriched—because I dared to prepare."

**Acknowledgement**

If the truth be told—and surely it must for this is a book about the truth of the pensions system and building pension wealth—then let me say plainly: no book is ever truly written alone. This one, least of all.

The book was born *after* retirement in 2023, in the restless hours when the world slept, but ideas and post-retirement flashbacks refused to. Night after night, I wrestled with words, chasing meaning through flickering thoughts, and a paper strewn study. I burned both ends of the candle and sometimes the middle too.

I lost count of the times I tip-toed into the bedroom only to wake Michele up with my clumsy attempts to crawl quietly into bed and be met with the inevitable "You're still alive then?".

Michele's unwavering interest in this book—and every time I disappeared into the spiral of rewrites—she brought me gently back with one simple prod: "Have you finished the book yet?"

To Michele—thank you for your constant support, the unwavering faith, and the love that anchored me through every silence. When words dried up or tiredness took hold, you were the quiet centre I returned to. Always.

Also, my deep gratitude to my son, Remmi, the savant with the brain of a planet who jointly came up with the title for the book after reading the draft and deep discussions into the night—on several nights! Not to forget my two girls, Kemmi Nastassia and Alexandra Zaria for their candid interests, burning curiosity and encouragement throughout. And last but not least to Joanna Penn of joanna@curluppress.com; you know who you are!

Finally, to the reader, thank you for choosing this book amid a world of hype and noise. If just one idea in this book helps you to either build pension wealth, avoid a fraudulent scam, make the right retirement income choices, or file a successful claim for compensation for poor service, then it was worth every keystroke.

With deep gratitude.

Yemmi Agbebi

## Dedication

To the Master, the navigating officers, the marine engineers, and the entire crew of the M.V. River Andoni—thrust into the melee of the 1979 Yokohama Typhoon, on her maiden crossing Westbound—We beat formidable odds!

This book stands in tribute to our seamanship and courage in a great tempest.

# Table of Contents

# Preface

## 0 To Build Wealth, Start Early. Earn More. Save More.

This book is for informational and educational purposes only. It's not meant to be taken as financial or pensions advice—because, well, it isn't. And while I hold an MBA and a Bachelor's degree equivalent in business law and nautical science, let me be absolutely clear: I have no business giving financial advice—and you can quote me on that!

What I do have though, is firsthand experience, knowledge, and expertise of growing my pension wealth to well over a £1 million—on a salary. In case you were wondering, no; this was not an accident. I planned it this way from age 23 and stayed the course. To put my pot in its proper context, according to a 2018 study by PensionBee, discounting north-south regional divide or differences, the average U.K pension pot is £21,441 source: https://www.pensionbee.com/uk/press/average-pension-pot.

Furthermore, with a portfolio of seven separate pension pots, I successfully navigated Britain's complex private and workplace pension purchase process for annuity and income drawdown. This book, with real life examples and templates, is an account of two halves—(a) how I built my pension wealth and (b) how I used that pot to secure a very comfortable retirement. And the really interesting part is this: anyone can copy what I did!

As I wrote this book, disturbing news of British nationals being scammed out of their life or pension savings came almost daily. Coming from a strong technology background, naturally, I've included a comprehensive yet easy-to-follow section on spotting online fraud, and scam prevention. Tackling this scourge was especially close to my heart given my former professional background in information technology and security. There's no need in this book to discuss the depth of my technology experience, however, it's worth skimming over what my background was.

I was CIO, Technology Director and a Senior Management Team (SMT) member at Manchester Airports Group. At Vodafone Global Enterprises, I was an information technology and telecommunications leader responsible for a £2.2 billion programme portfolio. Similarly, I led a global programme delivery team at Verizon Business with a typical programme value of £300 million. And last but not least, I was a Managing Principal Consultant and Technology Design Authority for global networks and data security at Siemens Professional Services. The chapter on anti-fraud alone is worth the price of the book.

Moving on, all too often, many people in the private sector assume their pension saving *is* their actual pension. Little do they realise that when they retire, they must buy a pension (annuity or income drawdown) with their savings. And while pension saving and pension purchase are interconnected, the two things are very different. Furthermore, in a climate where financial fraud and scams have reached epidemic proportions, converting pension savings into income is anything but a walk in the park.

Another common mistake is the wrong assumption that a large pension pot automatically translates into a good retirement income. This is not necessarily true because while a large pension pot is an excellent starting point, like any purchase or investment, the relationship between pension size and income is influenced by several critical factors like withdrawal strategy, inflation, taxation and so forth.

Indeed, sustained, high income in retirement depends largely on how wisely and effectively the pension pot was managed during the pension purchase process. Good planning, a flexible strategy, and regular reviews are what turns a big pension pot into a good life as the book shows.

So, not wanting to make the same costly financial mistakes as many individuals had, in January 2020, I began a thorough research of the internet—around three months before the COVID lockdown—for a book that would guide me through the pension purchase (or buying) process.

When I set out to find the book I *knew* was out there (it turned out I was wrong), I had three key criteria in mind. My foremost requirement was that the author had written from personal experience rather than theory—someone who had made the transition from pension saving to pension purchase. In other words, I was looking for an author who had gone through the pension purchase sausage machine and emerged battle-scarred but triumphant, with a wealth of lessons learnt under their belt.

The second criterion was that the book should contain real-world examples, useful tools, forms, templates, and other practical artefacts that I could borrow to help navigate the process. And the third benchmark was that the book had to be an easy read—not a heavy tome laden with jargon and tunnel vision, serving no real purpose.

In short, I was after a problem-solving or troubleshooting guide on pension wealth and purchase, not a theoretical work written by a Pollyanna. With these criteria in mind, I diligently trawled through Amazon UK, Waterstones, Google books, Goodreads, Barnes & Noble, and a few lesser-known platforms, searching for a publication that ticked all my boxes.

However, I drew a complete blank. Now, I would be lying if I said I didn't find plenty of books on pension wealth and retirement—in fact I did find several. However, not one was written by a retiree or an author who had "walked the walk" and truly understood the system from the inside.

The only books I came across were penned by pension and financial theorists, accountants, lawyers, financial advisers etc who described the process as it *should* work, not as it does in real life. Indeed, the overwhelming majority of books on the market dealing with pensions fell into one of two categories:

(a) books on pension saving and investment strategy, and
(b) books about what to do in retirement (e.g. hobbies, travel, etc).

No matter how hard I looked, I couldn't find a single book dedicated to the process of buying a pension—despite finding hundreds on how to save for a pension. Clearly, the nuanced difference between the two was either ignored by most authors or not widely understood.

Suffice to say, I was frustrated by my failure to find a suitable book. I had so many questions I wanted answered. For instance, I wanted to know what the lead time was from the start of the buying process to receipt of the first retirement income. I also wanted to know of any hacks that might facilitate a frictionless purchase, or how to get on the inside track to access the best available options.

Above all, I was determined to avoid dipping into my savings while my pension pots sat untouched in the providers' vaults, gathering dust and hopefully interest.

Moreover, virtually all the authors I came across were in their 30s, 40s, or early 50s. None, it seemed, was a retiree who had actually gone through the pension purchase process. The few who did touch on the subject painted a rosy picture grounded in theory and hearsay—but nothing else. Certainly, as I later discovered during my own retirement journey, their books were based neither on fact nor on personal experience.

Now, I do recognise the value that pension experts, tax specialists, financial advisers, and accountants bring to the table on specialist subjects like pension products, taxation, and legal frameworks.

Although, in reality, none of the authors I encountered had a clue what the nuts and bolts of pension buying were—whether for private, workplace, or stakeholder pensions. And while many understood the State Pension process well, that wasn't what I was looking for.

By the time I concluded my search, I came to realise that advice on pension purchase during the last five to ten years before retirement—the crucial transition or "sunset" years, when risks are at their highest—was largely absent. In other words, the countdown to retirement, or The Last Mile as I liked to call it, was not catered for.

Moreover, the vital window before retirement, during which pre-planning and transition from pension saving to purchase becomes critical, was left hanging in the air. There was no guidance whatsoever for people like me, whose retirement was imminent.

Now, I may be wrong, but at the time I suspected this gap wasn't due to a lack of interest. Rather, it likely stemmed from the fact that most authors writing about pensions had not yet made the transition from saving for a pension to actually buying one. As a result, they lacked first-hand experience, practical know-how, and nuanced understanding needed to write effectively about the pension buying process—which was as different from pension saving as light is from darkness.

Although I felt like a parcel for coming up empty-handed in my book search, I quietly resolved there and then, to write a talk-through and walk-through guide on pension wealth and purchase.

This is exactly what I've done in this book. In addition to detailing my own experience, knowledge gained, and lessons learnt, I've included pension buying examples and document templates to support a near-frictionless pension purchase experience.

I think I give nothing away when I state that a successful retirement begins with good planning, mental and emotional readiness. Retirement is a significant, life-changing event. Having a clear, robust transition plan to move from working life and pension wealth building to retirement was crucial to me—especially when having a plan could mean the difference between receiving pension income on time or enduring lengthy delays while depleting my backup savings.

Against this backdrop, I resolved from the outset to proactively plan and manage this approaching but crucial phase of my life diligently. Once retired, I understood that many things that I'd taken for granted over the last forty years would cease to be so. My clockwork salary would be no more. My lucrative annual bonus will be a thing of the past. Therefore, just as I had managed my career and earnings throughout my working life, I was determined to manage my transition to retirement just as successfully.

With this objective in mind, I felt it was crucial that I stepped into retirement with confidence and peace of mind, knowing that my financial future as a retiree was secure. However, this was only possible with prior planning, which began when I first caught the pension saving habit at 23 and ended with my retirement date set for 2023.

With twelve months left until retirement, I dived headlong into the pension purchase process with the goal that, when I finished my last day at work on Friday, 31 March 2023, my first pension income would land in my bank by 30 April 2023 without delay.

In the event, I was wrong. Contrary to what I had been led to believe by pension providers and the media, I discovered that, far from being a proficient, world-class industry, what I encountered was a woefully inefficient business model, operating in the full knowledge that it was 'too big to fail'.

Clearly, the impressions given by financial broadsheets, TV pundits, and tabloids about the ease of transitioning into retirement were not borne out by my experience—but more on that later. The issues I faced with pension providers were largely systemic and bore no resemblance to claims made in their brochures or in the financial press.

In fact, once I started my pension buying process, I realised very quickly that unless I was proactive and persistent in monitoring my application, I would be forced to dip into my savings to bridge the earnings gap between my last day at work and the receipt of my first pension income for around six months or more.

The only exceptions to my criticism of the pension industry were (a) the Department for Work and Pensions (DWP), for my frictionless State Pension, and (b) Standard Life for my workplace and stakeholder pensions. Both organisations were at the top of their game throughout and are to be highly commended.

Needless to say, I wrote this book to answer all the questions I wished I had answers to before embarking on my pension purchase process. Questions such as: What information, apart from my National Insurance (NI) number, will I need? What's the first step in the process and how long will it take? Was the process a slick, well-oiled machine or was it clunky and convoluted? What were the most common issues or challenges that I might face? Where were the 'alligators', and how would I avoid them?

Last but not least, throughout the book, I emphasised the importance of consulting professional financial advisers who are regulated and authorised to provide impartial financial and pension guidance. Speaking personally, seeking advice from authorised financial professionals regularly throughout my pension wealth journey has arguably been one of the best decisions I have made over the past forty years.

Moving on, the book began (Chapter 1) by describing how I built my pension wealth starting at the young age of 23, earning more, saving more and stock index investment. By the time I retired in 2023, I was literally pennies away from exceeding U.K.'s upper limit for pension savings or the Lifetime Allowance (LTA) of £1,073,100 (£1.07 million) during tax year 2023/2024. Importantly, my pension savings were separate and distinct from the value of my Index stocks or investments.

Chapter 2 evaluated the importance of taking professional advice from authorised financial planners and the importance of casting a critical eye on financial advice to ensure they're fit for purpose. Chapter 3 followed with a comprehensive overview of pension basics. This chapter provided a guided tour through the heartland pillars of U.K.'s pensions landscape.

To emphasize the interlock between the UK's pensions sector and regulation, Chapter 4 examined Britain's most influential pensions laws and legislation over the last 35 years or so. This chapter also set the format for the book overall, featuring several website links and useful telephone numbers. Overall, the book contains over 30 website links and an equal number of telephone numbers. This alone will save anyone with an interest in pensions, a lot of work and research.

Chapter 5 drew a distinction between accumulating wealth and decumulation or spending your wealth—which is about planning for retirement and how to spend the pot saved wisely and make it last a lifetime. The chapter also covered the emotional risks associated with retirement and proposed practical solutions for tackling them.

Chapter 6, 'Pension Success Blueprint' introduced planning tools, techniques and frameworks that a person purchasing a pension (buying annuity or entering drawdown), can use to rationalise the process for best and fast results.

Given the global scale of financial fraud in general and pension specific fraud in particular, it was inconceivable that a book on pension wealth and purchase wouldn't address this burning platform. Consequently, Chapter 7 was dedicated to analysing over thirty different kinds of frauds and scams, before outlining how to avoid falling victim to the myriads of swindles doing the rounds globally.

Chapter 8 explained the various categories of information (personal, NI record, GP health records, pension statements etc) that must be collated, collected and submitted in preparation for the pension buying process or for entering into drawdown. While Chapter 9 covered in great detail, the process of buying an annuity or entering drawdown, including website links, telephone numbers, other useful pension review and application information.

Chapters 10 and 11 described the importance of monitoring the progress status of the pension buying/drawdown process and why it's important to intervene when provider milestones or deadlines begin to drift. The chapters also explained how intervention could lead to substantial compensation in the event of serious delays traceable to the provider's operation. More pointedly, it described in full, how I used the techniques in this chapter to win five figure compensation from two pension providers. Chapter 11 features the actual email messages (redacted for sensitivity) exchanged between me, pension providers and the Ombudsman. This chapter also discussed the role, relevance and workings of the Office of the Ombudsman and described the right way and time to engage this consumer champion.

Chapter 12, 'Emotional Risks In Retirement', addressed an important area that's almost universally ignored in books dealing with building pension wealth in general and pensions in particular. Practical solutions on how to 'test drive' retirement before getting there and suggestions on dealing with the emotional baggage that sometimes comes with retirement.

In Chapter 13, the accumulated knowledge built up over my entire pension lifecycle (i.e. savings-buying a pension-decumulation etc) spanning over 40 years, was distilled down and presented in a practical and helpful manner using easily referenced format.

The book concluded with chapter 14, which analysed the challenges posed by the cost-of-living crisis to pensions and proposed practical solutions including contact telephone numbers, textphone numbers, websites and organisations through which a pensioner struggling with rising living costs can obtain help and assistance.

As a starter for ten, retirees affected by the cost-of-living crisis should check their eligibility for additional State benefits by contacting the following numbers: 🚨Pension Credit: Telephone 📞0800 99 1234 or Textphone 📞0800 169 0133.

For British residents over 50 and saving for a pension, Pension Wise is a free and impartial U.K. government service, offering guidance on a range of subjects concerned with pensions. 📌Pension Wise is contactable on 📞0800 731 0469

Finally, I wrote this book from a British perspective where I live, and which is arguably one of the most matured and oldest pension markets in the world. Indeed, the oldest pension company in the world is British; The Equitable Life Assurance Society, founded in 1762. It is now owned by Just Group plc, which acquired it in 2014. Even so, a significant swathe of the book applies to the other mature Anglophone countries comprising Australia, Canada, Eire (Ireland), New Zealand and the United States.

Indeed, all five countries PLUS Britain, operate similar legal frameworks and pension sectors. Consequently, it's not a stretch to draw a parallel with pensions between the U.K. and these five anglophone countries, given their past, shared history.

Last but not least, I've included in the book ready-to-use practical templates, simple formulas, forms, document examples, workplan examples, completed 'work instructions',—all gained from real-world, lived experience building my wealth and saving for retirement to subsequently buying a pension and entering income drawdown, living my best life!

## Chapter

## 1 Starting Early Vital For Building Pension Wealth

The Formula: Start Early. Earn More. Save More (SEEMSM)

### Bottom Line Up Front

I was 19 when I secured a coveted Navigating Officer Cadet place at the UK's premier School of Navigation, Warsash, Hampshire—then a college of the University of Southampton.

Early in the morning on my second day at Warsash and still in "finding my way around" mode, I got lost on my way to a lecture theatre that seemed determined not to be found!

Then, running slightly late for my naval architecture class, I stopped—standing at attention, as per college rules—to ask a senior officer cadet for help.

"Sir," I began, "I didn't mean to bother you, but—"

He cut me off mid-sentence.

"Well, you bloody have! How can I help? Make it quick, I'm on my way to a lecture, and 'Bottom Line Up Front'!"

For a moment, my mind was into a spin cycle, caught between processing his abrupt response and trying to decipher what he meant by 'Bottom Line Up Front'.

It was the first time I heard the term used or spoken by anyone.

Then, while in the middle of my inner turmoil, I had an epiphany: a thunderstruck moment—the meaning of his request became spontaneously clear! The senior officer cadet wanted me to lead with the crux of why I'd stopped him, and to leave the unnecessary details until last, preferably, not before he'd asked for further information.

**The Power of BLUF: Bottom Line Up Front**

In time, I would learn that BLUF, an acronym for "Bottom Line Up Front," is a communication technique that emphasizes delivering the most important information first and the non-essential details last.

Much like a crystal ball for the careful listener, BLUF allows one to cut through the verbal clutter and go straight to the chase, ensuring clarity and brevity.

Although at the time, I didn't realize just how far-reaching BLUF would influence the lens through which I saw the world.

**BLUF's Lasting Influence**

Despite the Officer Cadet's terse response knocking me off balance, initially, I didn't give our brief encounter any further thought—or so it seemed at the time. Although, in hindsight, BLUF made more of an impression on me than I first realized or dared to admit.

Over the following weeks and months, I frequently found myself reflecting on my 'BLUF encounter' and what it taught me about prioritisation and candidness.

After much deliberation, over time, I concluded that BLUF was a concept I could incorporate into both my written and oral communication style, and I did.

**BLUF: A Framework for Learning And Beyond**

With time, I recognized that BLUF's influence extended beyond mere communication.

✅ I developed oral and written communication style using BLUF.

✅ I used BLUF as a tool to master complex subjects—focusing on central concepts first before building on the details.

✅ I integrated BLUF into my social interactions, making discussions and presentations more structured and direct.

**BLUF and Pensions: Joining The Dots—Wealth & Intention**

Why is this important and what does BLUF have to do with pensions?

Bear with me while I park that question for a second—I will come back to it shortly.

After entering the world of work straight out of university, I adopted BLUF in meetings, report writing, business presentations and as the internet adoption gathered momentum, I used it in emails. Now, the reasons I'm telling you about BLUF are twofold:

✅ Firstly, I used BLUF to demonstrate how it influenced my pension savings habit at the young age of 23—but more on that later.

✅ Secondly, I combined BLUF with a concept called "Future History", an idea a former university friend shared with me after a chance meeting in 1978.

**Future History: A Game-Changing Thought Experiment**

It was late summer, 1978—in Liverpool. I ran into Richard, a former university friend, on Church Street, after a three-month hiatus following graduation. By the time we parted ways that afternoon, he had invited me to a BBQ at his house on the Wirral the following weekend; an invitation which I accepted.

From memory, there were around 15-20 guests at the BBQ, set in a mature back garden bursting with dazzling plants and three fairly mature trees. One of the trees was a Crab Apple, the second was a stunning Acer and the third tree escaped me.

As beer and barbecue flowed, small talk spread across the garden like Bluebells in April. By now, Richard had circulated his way to where I was standing, jigging to Boz Scaggs song and munching my way through a veggie kebab.

As we bantered about the size of the BBQ crowd and how many at the party looked like Easter Eggs, dressed in their summer colours. Then right out of the blue, Richard took me by surprise with an unexpected but almost weird question. At least that's what I thought at the time.

"Have you ever heard of a thought experiment called 'Future History'?" Richard asked.

I answered, "No. What's that?"

I assumed it was something he'd learned in his new role as a trainee actuary, but I didn't know for sure. "Future History," Richard began, "is when you visualize your future life in lucid Technicolor as though you were living it, in your 30s, 40s, 50s, 60s, 70s and beyond."

In my 20s, 30s, 40s, and 50s, my visualization histories went swimmingly, however when I reached my 60s, things became unclear—hazy, uncertain and fuzzy. I began to stutter and stammer—and couldn't get a single intelligible word out. As I struggled and hesitated for the right words, Richard interrupted my train of thought.

"I could sense a plot twist in your 60s" Richard began "things weren't as rosy as they were in the earlier decades, am I right?

I paused for a few seconds as I tried to find the right words before responding.

"Frankly, no! Life in my 60s had never before today been on my radar—ever! After all, I'm 23, and I've always imagined retirement at 65 was a 'million years' away!"

We both smiled, I nervously, and it was then that Richard dropped the kicker:

"OK, got it, So, you'll be 65 in a million years' time" he stifled another smile as he repeated my aphorism before carrying on. "By now, hopefully, you see that financial security at 65 and beyond starts with a decision today. To put it plainly, you must catch the savings bug—specifically, the pension savings habit—ASAP.

Bottomline, otherwise, the golden years you envision may come to an abrupt and disappointing end when you retire."

"It was a rhetorical statement, but it hit the bullseye! I paused for a few seconds, reflecting on Richard's words, then responded in a measured, low voice—what would ultimately become the defining moment of my pension wealth strategy.

“Sure, I get it", I spoke slowly. "Retirement is the ultimate bottom-line-up-first (BLUF) event—the culmination of everything that came before”. I paused briefly to collect my thoughts: “Look, everything I have ever done in my life—every decision, every sacrifice—was, in its own way, preparation for what lay ahead. It all led me to this point: wealth in retirement or mere existence”. I decided there and then that I would enter retirement not diminished, not haunted by the regret of failing to plan, but enriched—because I dared to prepare.

Up until that point, I had felt vulnerable about old age and uncertain about retirement. Yet, lurking within that acorn of uncertainty was a newfound clarity—an epiphany on what I must do to secure my retirement. I must start saving into a pension immediately.

And that was exactly what I did. Perhaps it was Richard's reference to 'bottom line' that reignited BLUF in my mind. I don't know.

Although I knew instantly from that point onwards what I must do.

**Figure 1.0 Future History - The Evolution of Ageing**

**Bottom Line Up First (BLUF):**

✅ Start Early. Earn More. Save More (**SEEMSM**) pronounced 'Simpsom)

✅ Prioritize retirement wealth as a non-negotiable objective

BLUF—my faithful North Star—has once again guided me home! That moment of clarity was like 'The Great Unveiling'. It revealed to me the undeniable connection between a wealthy retirement and early pension savings.

So, when was the best time to start saving for a pension? Forty years ago. When is the next best time? Today! Over the next 45 years, I built up seven substantial pension pots, stock index—plus State pension. I was determined to secure my life in retirement because the alternative was not palatable.

**SEEMSM - Building Pension Wealth Code Over Five Decades**

My Pension Code SEEMSM was a collection of doctrines developed over time to guide my approach to building affluence and pension wealth during my working life. It goes without saying that I always sought professional financial advice from certified planners. Central to the Code was the "starting early" savings doctrine underpinned by "earn more, save more and invest in an Index"—a good foundation for building wealth as I subsequently discovered.

Whether SEEMSM is distilled down into its individual essence or seen holistically, it is without doubt a virtuous cycle of activities, with each doctrine feeding into the next and so on, until it becomes a wealth creation engine. Let me explain how. At a practical level, SEEMSM begins with starting early (i.e. saving), but, unless you're earning considerably more money than the cost of meeting your essentials (i.e. housing, bills, food etc) and discretionary spend (i.e. clothing, gifts, vacations etc), it's highly unlikely you'll have much money left to save, if at all.

Therefore, despite how the acronym in the code is ordered, 'Earn More' self-selects as the first among equals, because it is the only doctrine which guarantees all the others in the Code.

Thus, if we crank the model, the result should read something like this: "if you earn more, it's easier to start a savings habit quickly and the more money you earn, the more you can save into a pension as well as into an investment or wealth portfolio". Are you with me? It's important that you are. 'Earning More' became a healthy addiction that I fed, and later on in this chapter, I described exactly how I did that without laying out a penny. That was something else I avoided—throwing good money after bad.

To give SEEMSM life and make it an easily implementable and practical wealth building framework, I distilled the Code into seven 'Must Do'—all interconnected which are discussed in more detail below.

**a. Boost Employer Matching Contributions (Earn/Save More)**

Pension matching or enhanced employer contributions is a valuable incentive where employers contribute significantly more than the legal minimum to an employee's workplace pension. Contributions increase when the employee agrees to boost their pension contributions, effectively growing their retirement funds faster.

Boosting is a smart financial move to maximize pension savings because a 'boost' is literally free money!

**b. Subscribe to a Salary Sacrifice Scheme (Save/More)**

Salary sacrifice is when an employee voluntarily agrees to a reduction in their gross salary—typically reflected as a deduction on their payslip—in exchange for their employer paying the reduction directly into their workplace pension. It's a win-win, as both the employee and employer benefit from tax and National Insurance savings, making it an efficient way to boost pension contributions while lowering taxable income.

**c. Supplement Pot with Performance Bonus (Save/More)**

Supplementing a pension pot involves making an annual, one-off lump-sum contribution into retirement savings, typically from a matured ISA or proceeds of stocks divestment. In my particular case, I opted to have my annual performance bonuses paid directly into my pension rather than receiving it as taxable income. This prudent choice not only strengthened my retirement savings pot but also provided tax and National Insurance savings for both my employer and me. Moreover, performance bonus supplementation also enjoys additional tax benefits and advantages which are covered in sub-section (d) below.

### d. Maximise Tax Relief on Performance Bonus (Save/More)

Tax relief on performance bonus, is a specific type of pension supplementation. However, it differs significantly from ISA and other types of one-off, lump sum supplementation because of its inherent tax advantages. Quite apart from tax and NI savings, when an annual performance bonus is paid directly into a pension, it is boosted by tax relief of between 20% and 45%, depending on an individual's Income tax rate. The same principle applies to salary sacrifice and additional voluntary contributions (AVCs).

### e. Invest In a Stock Index e.g. S&P 500 NOT Individual Stocks

On the advice of my financial planner, I invested in a stocks index like the S&P 500, DAX (DE40), Nikkei 225 rather than ISAs, because the former provided me with three unmatched, compelling financial benefits not least peace of mind:

(a) instant diversification across leading multinationals reducing stock risks.

(b) Decades of evidence that indexes consistently outperform most actively managed funds over time due to lower fees and broad market exposure.

(c) It was a simple, cost-effective way to build wealth while benefiting from compound interest returns, economic growth and market resilience.

A 2018 study by the Index Industry Association (IIA) estimated there were approximately 3.3 million stock market indices worldwide. With such a packed field, I chose to focus my investments on one of the Top 10 or so leading global financial indices, but especially the following top five indices.

1. **S&P 500** – Represents 500 of the largest U.S. companies, offering broad market exposure.
2. **NASDAQ-100** – Focuses on 100 leading non-financial companies, mostly in technology.
3. **Dow Jones Industrial Average** – Tracks 30 significant U.S. companies across various industries.
4. **FTSE 100** – The 100 largest firms listed on the London Stock Exchange.
5. **Nikkei 225** – Japan's top 225 firms trading on the Tokyo Stock Exchange.

### f. Pursue Age-Correlated Salary Targets (Earn More)

In my late 20s, I set myself age-related salary targets for each decade (i.e. 20s, 30s, 40s, 50s and 60s) of my professional career. I first encountered this salary criterion in *a management article I came across around the age of 25* and since that time, I pursued these targets rigorously throughout my working life.

Age-correlated salary is calculated by multiplying a variable multiplier (ranging from 2.0 to 3.0) by a person's age and then by £1,000 as in the following example:

Age-correlated salary: 2.0 × 30 years × £1,000 = £60,000 salary target at age 30. This table shows examples of age-related salary targets from age 30-60, which I created over 40 years ago.

It became my Bible whenever I negotiated a pay rise or moved into a new role. Throughout my career from age 30 onwards, the trajectory of my salaries unwaveringly tracked the 2.0 to 3.0 multipliers.

**Figure 2.0 Age Correlated Salary Targets**

| **Age** | **2.0 x Age x £1000** | **2.5 x Age x £1000** | **3.0 x Age x £1000** |
|---|---|---|---|
| **30 years old** | £60,000 | £75,000 | £90,000 |
| **40 years old** | £80,000 | £100,000 | £120,000 |
| **50 years old** | £100,000 | £125,000 | £150,000 |
| **60 years old** | £120,000 | £150,000 | £180,000 |

On the following page in Figure 3.0, I've included my HMRC tax demand for underpaid income tax in the financial year 2021–22. The demand details several key figures. For instance, my total earnings for the year were £179,811, and my PAYE tax deductions came to £64,899.95, leaving an underpayment of £2,320.95, which I subsequently settled after receiving the featured tax demand.

A quick run through of the tax demand shows the following: in the top left-hand corner of the demand is my name, and in the top right-hand corner is my Unique Tax Reference (UTR). As you would expect, I've redacted my UTR for personal identity security reasons and as an anti-fraud measure. Indeed, in this book, I've dedicated an entire chapter to analyse and provide tried and tested solutions, to tackle identity theft, fraudulent scams and pension scams.

Now, before I lose my train of thought on age-correlated salary targets using multipliers, let me back-up for a moment to my tax demand and what it reveals about my earnings in the 2021/22 tax year. Using the figures provided by HMRC, I calculated my age-related salary multiplier as 2.74 points—just 0.26 points short of my target annual salary multiplier of 3.0 at that age. Although, had my performance bonus been added to my earnings instead of my pension pot, I would have topped out at 3.4 multiplier. Here's a challenge for you: Can you work out how old I was in 2022?

**Figure 3.0 HMRC Tax Demand 2021/22**

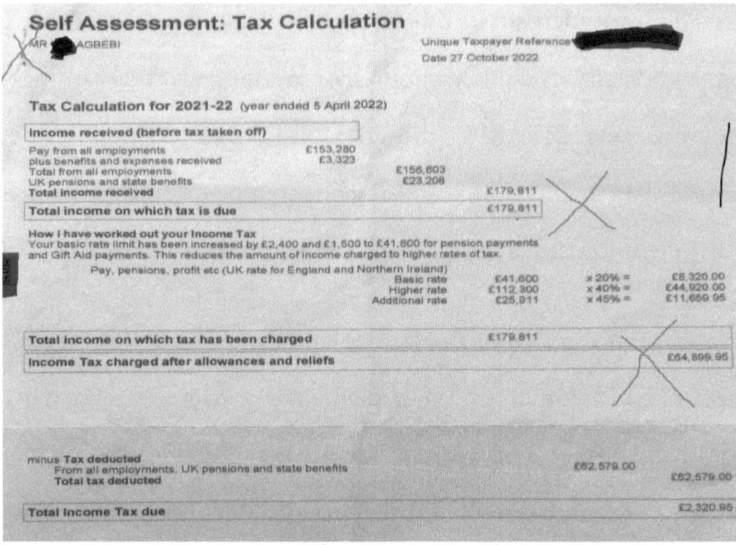

Self Assessment: Tax Calculation

MR AGBEBI

Unique Taxpayer Reference

Date 27 October 2022

Tax Calculation for 2021-22 (year ended 5 April 2022)

| Income received (before tax taken off) | | | |
|---|---|---|---|
| Pay from all employments | £153,280 | | |
| plus benefits and expenses received | £3,323 | | |
| Total from all employments | | £156,603 | |
| UK pensions and state benefits | | £23,208 | |
| Total income received | | | £179,811 |
| Total income on which tax is due | | | £179,811 |

How I have worked out your Income Tax
Your basic rate limit has been increased by £2,400 and £1,500 to £41,600 for pension payments and Gift Aid payments. This reduces the amount of income charged to higher rates of tax.

Pay, pensions, profit etc (UK rate for England and Northern Ireland)

| | | | |
|---|---|---|---|
| Basic rate | £41,600 | x 20% = | £8,320.00 |
| Higher rate | £112,300 | x 40% = | £44,920.00 |
| Additional rate | £25,911 | x 45% = | £11,659.95 |

| | | |
|---|---|---|
| Total income on which tax has been charged | £179,811 | |
| Income Tax charged after allowances and reliefs | | £64,899.95 |
| minus Tax deducted | | |
| From all employments, UK pensions and state benefits | £62,579.00 | |
| Total tax deducted | | £62,579.00 |
| Total Income Tax due | | £2,320.95 |

Starting in my 20s and continuing through my 30s, 40s, 50s, and into my 60s, I applied the pertinent aspects of my Pension Code—its doctrines—on a decade-by-decade basis. My principal doctrine was to grow my earnings at every opportunity and by association, my pension pots.

## G. Pension Pot Target (PPT) By Decade Starting In My 20s

In the same manner that I developed age-related salary targets for each working decade (i.e., 20s, 30s, 40s, 50s, and 60s), I created SMART—Specific, Measurable, Achievable, Realistic and Time-bound—pension pot targets, to track and monitor the status of my retirement wealth over five or six decades.

It's true, isn't it, that what you can't measure (e.g. size of pension pot), you can't manage (i.e. make choices or decisions, etc)—and what you can't manage, you can't improve (i.e. save more and/or change investment strategy to grow wealth faster).

Rightly or wrongly, a person's pension pot and lived experience in retirement is highly correlated to the earning power of that individual during their working life, as PensionBee's 2018 study referenced in the preface demonstrated.

Consequently, setting a target PTT, combined with good planning and intention and periodic review of the size of the pot is crucial.

This approach to building pension wealth in retirement is not unlike one of the management methods used to control and improve outcomes either over the short, medium and long term called Plan-Do-Check-Act (PDCA).

PDCA is a four-step iterative process for continuous improvement of an output, except in this case the output was my pension pot target. The Plan-Do-Check-Act concept is illustrated in Figure 4.0 below.

**Figure 4.0 HMRC Tax Demand 2021/22**

**Plan-Do-Check-Act Continuous Improvement Framework**

As this book went to press, the U.K. Labour Cabinet minister Liz Kendall warned that British pensioners face a *'tsunami of poverty'* as workers 'are not saving enough for retirement'. Consequently, she announced a review of the retirement age as she launched a new pension commission to head the review.

Her comments were the latest evidence the British pension system is far from being fit for purpose;—leaving the British workforce with the distinct impression that it was their responsibility to shape their own destiny in retirement—or otherwise suffer the consequences.

Faced by this daunting challenge, elements of SEEMSM (e.g. age-related salaries etc) when combined with pension pot targets over many decades, is a robust way of ensuring a person's retirement pot remains on track to deliver a comfortable life in their 60s.

Setting pension pot targets by age is a smart way to track progress and stay motivated. Here's the framework I used after taking advice from a financial adviser in my mid-20s.

**Figure 5.0 Pension Pot Target By Age**

| Age | Pension Pot Target | Inflation* | Observation |
|---|---|---|---|
| **20s** | 0.5* x Annual Salary | Included in the multiple (x0.5) | Start Early |
| **30s** | 1* x Annual Salary | Included in the multiple (x1) | Earn More |
| **40s** | 3* x Annual Salary | Included in the multiple (x3) | Save More |
| **50s** | 6* x Annual Salary | Included in the multiple (x6) | Review/Adjust |
| **60s** | 9* x Annual Salary | Included in the multiple (x9) | Safeguard and Retire |

For example, if your current salary is £40,000, depending on how old you are, all things being equal your pension pot targets would be:

- £20,000 - if in your 20s
- £40,000 - if in your 30s
- £120,000 - if in your 40s
- £240,000 - if in your 50s
- £360,000 - in your 60s

A comfortable retirement was never going to be handed to you or anyone else on a silver plate. It's down to you to build it. This book describes in great detail how I built my affluence and pension wealth. Purposed intention, allied with the SEEMSM framework, is a very good place to start and it's exactly what I did. And if I can do it, so can anybody.

**Evolution of Start Early-Earn-More-Save-More over 50 years**

The Information below is organized into five thematic parts, covering approximately five decades of employment, beginning in 1978. For each decade, I've created a clear and easily digestible "Must-Do List" from the SEEMSM Code, highlighting the doctrines I adopted and, where practicable, the reasons why.

At this point, I should clarify that although I've listed the Code I lived by below, these lists do not constitute financial advice.

Rather, they reflect my personal experiences as I progressed through the decades during my working life.

To say the Code was instrumental in building my pension wealth across the decades is an understatement. The code played no less a part than a coastal lighthouse does for a ship at night or in foggy conditions. It lit my way and guided me through tough times like when I was seriously tempted to reduce my monthly pension contribution from 15% to single figures or divest of an Index stock and so forth.

SEEMSM, the salary and pension pot targets became visual navigational aids that ensured I remained on course over four decades, with my eyes firmly fixed on my final port of destination: pension wealth in retirement.

### 📌My 20s: Laid The Foundation By Starting Early

My 20s were about forming a regular savings habit and sticking to it—come hell or high water. This savings habit laid the foundation for my pension pots in later years.

The doctrines I adopted in my 20s functioned like jigsaw pieces, coming together to form a comprehensive financial strategy.

- **Savings Habit:** Prioritizing regular savings. I budgeted small but constant and consistent contributions to give my pension pot a head start and a solid baseline.
- **Start Early:** I started saving as soon as I began earning, following my *Future History* encounter on the Wirral. I had high hopes that the magic of compound interest would, over time, work wonders for my savings.
- **Automatic Enrolment:** I enrolled in workplace pensions as soon as I was eligible, usually following a probationary period. My employers' pension contributions to my pot were essentially highly coveted free money.
- **Stock Index Investment:** Invested in a stock that tracked a specific stock market index, rather than individual stocks—funds that mirrored the composition and performance of a given index over at least 30+ years.

### 📌My 30s: Built Momentum, Diversified and Earned an MBA

While my 20s were about gaining a head start and forming a regular savings habit, in my 30s, I focused on building momentum to grow my pension and wealth. Firstly, I set myself the goal of achieving executive-level education with a view to boost my earnings. Accordingly, I earned a Master of Business Administration (MBA) from the University of Keele, Staffordshire, which opened new career doors and led to higher salaries.

Finally, after consulting several Regulated financial professionals for free advice, I diversified my investment portfolio.

- **Executive Education:** I enrolled in a two-year MBA program at the University of Keele to enhance my career prospects and earnings potential. Increased earnings meant higher pension savings and bigger employer contributions to my pension pot.
- **Age-Correlated Salary Targets:** After successfully completing my MBA, I set a salary target using a multiplier of 2.0 throughout my 30s. For example, at 35, this worked out as 2.0 × 35 yrs × £1,000 = £70,000 salary target.
- **Increased Contributions:**
    1. I took out an Additional Voluntary Contribution (AVC) or a personal pension savings scheme.
    2. I opted for my employers' salary sacrifice scheme to improve my pension pot's tax efficiency.
- **Diversified Investments:** I took an active interest in managing my with-profits pension savings. For the first time since I started saving, I diversified my portfolio to minimize risk and increase investment returns.

- **Stock Index Investment:** Invested in a stock that tracked a specific stock market index, rather than individual stocks—funds that mirrored the composition and performance of a given index over at least 30+ years.

### 📌My 40s: Maximized Pension Pot Values & Salary Multiples

By my early 40s, I had been saving for over twenty years, and my pension pots (now four in total) had grown substantially. The salary sacrifices I made in my mid-30s had paid off significantly. Additionally, I set a target salary multiplier of 2.5 throughout my 40s. This formula was consistent across my 30s, 40s, 50s, and 60s—the only variable was the multiplier, which could be 2.0, 2.5, 2.75, or 3.0.

**Investments Reviewed and Adjusted:** I regularly reviewed and adjusted my pension plans (i.e., funds) to ensure optimal growth.

- **Increased Contributions:** Although I had not yet reached the peak of my earning power (which came in my 50s and 60s), I increased my AVC to take advantage of tax relief. Additionally, depending on the legal upper limit, I allocated a large proportion—or all—of my annual performance bonus into my pension pot, benefiting from extra tax relief. Lastly, by maximizing my workplace savings, I increased the amount of matched contributions that my employers made.

- **Achieved Compensation/Salary Target:** In my 40s, I set an annual salary target equivalent to 2.5 × £1,000 for every year of age. For example, at 40 years old, my salary target was: 2.5 × 40 × £1,000 = £100,000
- **Stock Index Investment:** Invested in a stock that tracked a specific stock market index, rather than individual stocks—funds that mirrored the composition and performance of a given index over at least 30+ years.

### 📌My 50s: Accelerated Growth and Lowered Risk Profile

I spent my 50s aggressively increasing my annual compensation (i.e., salaries), which in turn allowed me to save more for retirement.

This included securing increased tax relief and maximizing employer contributions to my workplace pension. Each of these doctrines contributed to growing the amount of money going into my pots.

- **Achieved Compensation/Salary Target:** In my 50s, I set an annual salary target equivalent to 3 × £1,000 for every year of age. For example, my salary target at age 50 was: 3 × 50 × £1,000 = £150,000.
- **Increased Contributions:** Depending on the prevailing legal upper limit, I allocated all or part of my annual performance bonus into my pension and benefited from additional tax relief.

- **Reduced Portfolio Risk Profile:** From age 55, I gradually shifted my investments toward lower-risk options to safeguard my savings from market shocks and volatility.
- **Pension Basics and Retirement Options Refresher:** At age 59, I requested a *retirement wake-up pack* from my provider and began formulating a basic *Transition to Retirement* plan. I immersed myself in learning about the following subjects:- pensions in general and *Drawdown vs. Annuity* in particular.
- **Stock Index Investment:** Invested in a stock that tracked a specific stock market index, rather than individual stocks—funds that mirrored the composition and performance of a given index over at least 30+ years.

### My 60s: Pivoted To Safety, Security & Transition Planning

Firstly, I applied the standard doctrines that had served me well over 40 years of savings—these included age-related compensation targets, pension boost strategies, and tax relief optimization.

Secondly, I spent my 60s securing my pension pots to prevent falling victim to scams or fraud. Having invested decades into building my savings, I had no intention of losing it with the finish line so close!

- **Moved pots to Lower-Risk Investments:** I transitioned all funds in my pension pots to low-risk or lower-risk investments, which I monitored electronically on a weekly—sometimes daily—basis.
- **Implemented a Pension Transfer Embargo:** To shield my savings from scams and fraud, I strictly prohibited transferring or moving my pension pots between providers. This ensured my savings remained secure.
- **Stock Index Investment:** Invested in stocks that tracked a stock market index, rather than individual stocks—funds that mirrored the composition and performance of a given index over at least 30+ years. e.g. FTSE 100, S&P 500 etc.

Lastly, I initiated a series of pension-buying and transition transfer activities, in preparation for retirement. These were as follows:-

### 📌Finalizing My Retirement Strategy

**Finalized My Retirement and Pensions Transition Plan**: The transition-to-retirement plan that I developed became the foundation for this book. I documented and reviewed my retirement plan, making final adjustments as needed.

- **Checked My HMRC National Insurance (NI) Record:** I reviewed my HMRC NI record to ensure I had accumulated sufficient qualifying years for the full New State Pension. *Check yours now:* 🔗 *https://www.gov.uk/check-national-insurance-record)*

- **Analyzed and Evaluated Drawdown vs. Annuities:** I explored annuity and drawdown options to ensure I was fully informed about which approach was best suited to my lifestyle. My goal was to secure a regular and stable whole-life income stream in retirement with a drawdown pot as a reserve.
- **Triggered the Pension Buying Process**: I initiated my pension-buying process well in advance to ensure it aligned with my retirement date.
- **Reviewed Latest Headline Pension Guidance**: I updated myself with basic headline pensions and tax laws guidance that might affect my retirement plans. For example, the

Lifetime Allowance (LTA) was abolished in April 2024, a mere one year after my retirement.

**Reflecting on My Code/Doctrines To Build Pension Wealth**

I think it's fair to say the Pension Code and doctrines which I first developed at age 23, guided my working life affluence and pension strategy until retirement in 2023. Of course, as each decade emerged, they came with their set of unique challenges. These were mere changes in the direction of the overarching current and I adjusted the course of my doctrines and code accordingly. Notwithstanding, the core or the heartlands of the code remained unchanged.

Of course, when I was 23, I didn't know what I didn't know (*i.e. unknown unknowns*)—such as what I would be earning in my 30s, 40s, 50s and beyond. However, using the age-related earnings formula that I described earlier, I had a pretty good idea what my salary targets were, and I pursued these relentlessly!

Additionally, from my early 20s, I had a clear vision of the kind of lifestyle that I wanted in retirement, and I diligently managed my career aspirations to this end.

## Chapter

# 2 Taking Financial Advice

Good Advice Is Your Best Friend. Bad Advice Is Your Worst Enemy

### Bottom Line Up Front

Regardless of what you might have been told, read or seen in the mainstream or social media reels, building wealth is a skill that must be learnt and taking sound financial advice from certified financial professionals is the best starting point.

In parallel with building wealth (i.e. start early, earn more, save more and invest in an Index), scanning your retirement horizon, having a formal retirement plan allowed me to set objectives, prioritize tasks, schedule activities, and manage risks, even as I navigated my way through mastering building pension wealth.

Furthermore, planning enabled me to identify and anticipate potential risks, reduce uncertainty, and adapt more easily to changing circumstances. It was like creating a roadmap from A to Z—giving me a line of sight and clarity on where I was heading, how much progress remained, and how to avoid getting lost along the way. To summarize, planning became the crucial bedrock and foundation on which I built my pension purchase strategy, using my pension pots.

## Retirement Transition

### Taking Financial Advice Before Kicking Things Off

A fundamental step prior to starting my transition planning was to schedule four separate meetings with one of my pension providers, where I was allocated a Personal Account Manager—a reflection of the size of my pension portfolio.

Additionally, these scheduled meetings were supplemented by two online Zoom conferences on pension-related topics. This planning phase began as I entered my five-year ramping-down window towards retirement.

I should clarify that while my pension provider did not offer advice, they provided an immense amount of information that proved invaluable in my decision-making process. I cannot overemphasize how essential I found these provider facilitated sessions. The 1-2-1 meetings and conferences helped me to:

✅ Understand my options and relevant choices.

✅ Evaluate potential fees and tax implications.

✅ Update and upskill myself on the latest govt legislation and guidelines.

**Making My Pension Choice**

By the time I finally retired, I had made my pension decisions like a well-oiled machine—thanks to the time invested in meetings with financial advisers and teleconferences on pensions to thoroughly understand pension planning, my options, potential pitfalls and the inherent tax implications of various options.

Among the seven providers I saved with—alongside the State Pension, which I will discuss later—some providers stood out for their competence and support.

✅ **Standard Life** – Exceptionally helpful, supportive, informative, and administratively competent throughout the process.

✅ **Scottish Widows** – A provider I highly rate for customer support and efficiency.

The above statements should not be construed as a recommendation of the providers mentioned. My comments are strictly well-deserved recognition for two private providers and the Pension Office of the DWP, that are exemplars of outstanding customer service and proficient business operations.

## Taking Financial Advice

From the start of my working life, seeking out financial advice from FCA-regulated advisers, was one of the smartest decisions I made in retrospect.

Without a shadow of a doubt, correct financial advice is one of the two bedrocks of financial security in retirement.

The other? Saving regularly, constantly and consistently for a pension throughout my career, taking care not to miss a heartbeat!

Early in my career, I made the commitment to save as much money as possible plus a little bit more, constrained only by prevailing pension regulations.

This commitment was largely influenced by my chance encounter with the 'Future History' thought experiment, which I discussed fully in an earlier chapter.

In my thought experiment, I was determined that I would not end up a basket case in old-age pensioners (OAP)—either living on the breadline or forced to cut back drastically in retirement.

Particularly with the challenges of old age such as they are, not least the inevitable decline in physical wellbeing, cognitive abilities, and an increased risk of chronic health conditions that loomed large in old age.

With this in mind, I proactively met with multiple financial advisers—starting at age 23 and continuing throughout my professional career—to seek their expertise on pension planning.

**Consulting Tier 1 Pension Providers**

Throughout my career, I held numerous meetings with some of the leading Tier 1 pension providers, including:

✅ Legal & General

✅ Standard Life

✅ Scottish Widows

✅ Pension Wise (*UK Govt. agency–contact:* 📞*0800 138 3944*)

The net result of these consultations was access to expert wealth advice and an abundance of information from regulated and certified professionals, regarding the various pension schemes and investment options available to me.

## The Value of Financial Advice—And Its Limitations

Taken altogether, the vast majority of the financial advice that I received was helpful and ultimately informed the choices I made when saving for retirement, but notably, when using my pension savings to buy a pension in retirement.

As is almost always the case, there are two sides to every story, and I would be remiss if I claimed that all the professional guidance I received was sound advice.

However, before I disappear down the good, the bad and the ugly warren, I would like to paint regulated financial advice and advisers in their proper and correct light. Although it's important to bear in mind that in all walks of life, there are good and not so good individuals in every profession.

For example, one only has to look at the register of the U.K's General Medical Council, for the list of doctors struck off for professional misconduct. That said, most professionals in any industry are by and large competent and trustworthy.

## Financial Advice Is Indispensable When Saving for a Pension

Engaging a financial adviser for planning is not an event; it is a process. Mine began at age 23 and continued right up to the point when I chose to retire in my 60s.

Financial advisers specialising in pensions laws and regulations are crucial, because navigating pension planning requires expertise in tax, law, and finance—a trifecta where a qualified financial adviser can prove invaluable.

Advisers can bring their expertise to bear in these specialist areas when advising pension savers, including individuals approaching retirement. This is a matter that should engage anyone who is saving into a pension scheme.

**1. Decoding Complexity of Pension Rules**

Pension regulations are intricate and constantly evolving. It is not unusual for savers and those approaching retirement to be tripped up by the fast-shifting quicksand of legislation, contribution limits, or withdrawal rules. Advisers decode these complexities, ensuring compliance and optimising benefits for savers.

**2. Tax Efficiency**

An adviser's scrutiny can reveal and unravel how pensions intersect and interlock with taxation regulations. Good advisers structure contributions to take advantage of tax reliefs (e.g. income tax relief on contributions) while mitigating liabilities, such as LTA or inheritance tax pitfalls.

**3. Tailored Investment Strategy**

Because pension saving pots could span several decades; poor investment choices over a long time can erode growth. Advisers can align portfolios with an individual's risk appetite, retirement goals, and market directions, adjusting strategies as circumstances evolve.

**4. End-to-End Planning**

Strictly speaking, an adviser's planning role might extend beyond pensions. Advisers can integrate retirement savings with wider wealth—property, stocks, ISAs or inheritance plans—to create balanced but diversified income strategies.

**5. Avoiding Costly Mistakes**

From unsuitable drawdown choices to underestimating longevity risks, pension missteps are unfortunately irreversible. Advisers provide foresight, safeguarding against costly financial errors that could derail retirement security.

In short, an adviser combines technical knowledge with personalised guidance, reshaping pension savings from a gamble into a calculated, tax-efficient roadmap. Their value? Peace of mind that your financial future is secured.

### Two Bad Financial Advice Ignored

By the time I reached retirement, I had accumulated seven additional pension pots from past employment, resulting in a total of eight pension pots including the State Pension.

This portfolio brought me dangerously close to the Lifetime Allowance (LTA) limit of £1,073,100 (£1.07 million), which was in force at the time.

Although, as of 6 April 2024, the LTA was abolished, meaning there's no longer a maximum cap or upper limit on the amount that individuals could save in their pension pots.

It's important to clarify that UK pension providers are not usually authorised to provide financial advice—though they can provide information.

Therefore, to be crystal clear: none of my pension providers that I saved with, were involved in the bad advice that I am about to describe.

**Figure 6.0 Pension Wise Example - Know Your Options**

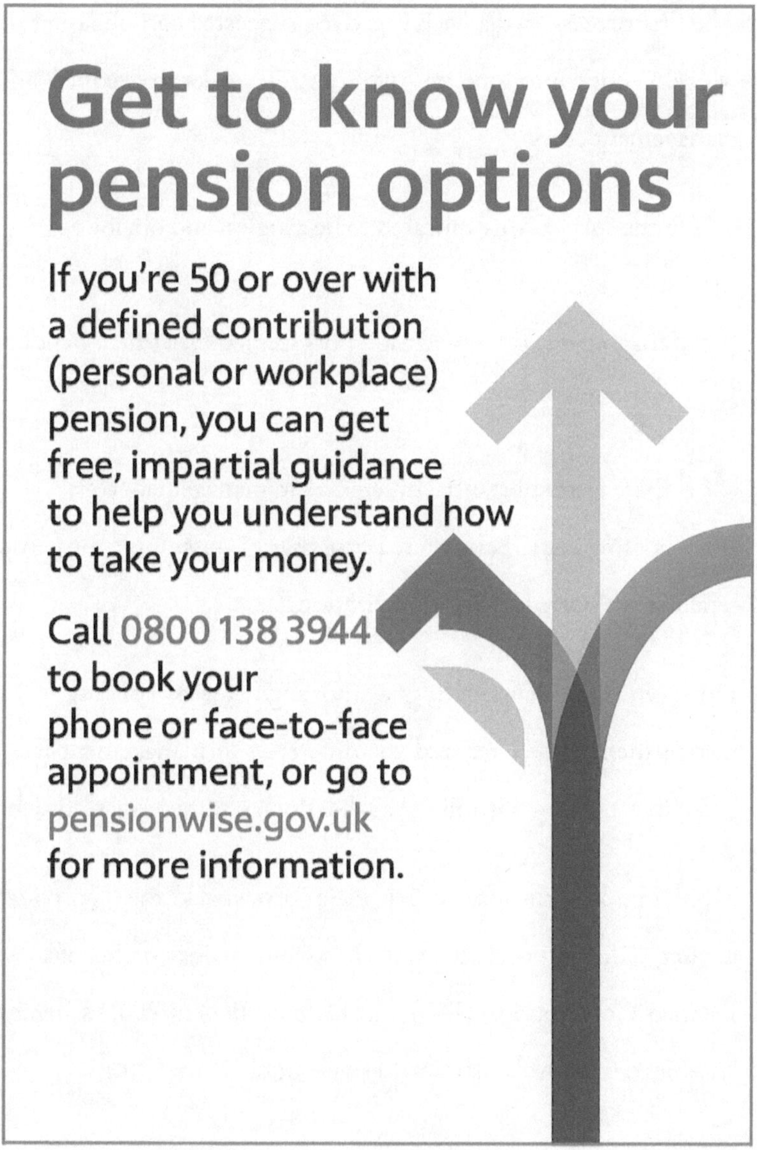

**Bad Advice #1: Consolidating My Pension Pots**

The first professional advice I received suggested consolidating all my pension pots into one or two pots in order to reduce annual management costs.

📌On the surface, this appeared to be a logical and obvious suggestion:

✅ Managing one or two pension pots seemed easier than handling eight.

✅ If there were substantial differences in management fees, consolidating could have offered cost savings—assuming my pension schemes supported such rationalization.

However, after conducting a thorough review of my pension management fees, I realized the difference in management fees was negligible, making portfolio consolidation an unnecessary burden.

More importantly, one other major drawback the consolidation adviser failed to consider was the potential loss of benefits when Defined Contribution (DC) and Defined Benefit (DB) schemes are combined or consolidated into a single pot.

Combining the two different schemes was akin to mixing oil and water—no, it's worse than that! It was more like dropping potassium

(K) element-19into water, triggering an explosive reaction, as you might recall from Year 7 Chemistry experiments.

📌 **And here's why:**

✅ Defined Benefit (DB) pensions are calculated based on final salary, years of service, and a multiplier formula unique to the employer.

✅ Defined Contribution (DC) pensions rely solely on investment performance.

Had I rushed into consolidating my DB and DC schemes, I would have suffered significant financial losses and benefits, specifically protection against inflation, both immediately and in the long term.

Fortunately, many pension providers refuse to merge DB and DC plans—a policy that saved me from making a costly mistake when I inadvertently tried to combine one of my DB schemes with a DC plan while in the process of buying an annuity.

Furthermore, consolidating my high-return pension schemes would have delayed my first pension payment by six months—causing me to miss out on income in excess of £30,000.

Despite giving serious thought to consolidation, after weighing the benefits against the pitfalls, I ultimately decided against doing so.

Buying a pension neither comes with a step-by-step guide nor does it come with a fixed guaranteed date when the pension income tap will be turned on. Fortunately, I had ring-fenced over £40,000 in savings to cover contingencies in case of delays to my pension income—which, unfortunately, did happen.

While some providers began paying out six weeks after my final purchase submission, the worst provider took six months.

Had I followed the consolidation advice, I would have faced serious disruption in my financial affairs—thankfully I avoided this outcome because I ignored what I thought was bad financial advice.

**Bad Advice #2: Avoiding Additional Voluntary Contributions**

The second bad advice that I received related to private Additional Voluntary Contributions (AVCs). To my surprise, three out of four advisors advised against taking out a private AVC because of the following reasons viz:-

❌ "...You might not benefit from the full amount, as some of it will be deducted for income tax."

❌ "...Boosting your pension income could affect entitlements to means-tested benefits."

In my particular circumstances both arguments were flawed—and they immediately set off the following red flags in my mind.

### 🚩 Red Flag #1: Means-Tested Benefits

This was irrelevant to my financial plan—claiming social benefits in retirement was never on the cards due to the size of my pots. Both planners had this information and yet this was the advice I received.

Indeed, my strong aversion to reliance on benefits in old age was the main reason why I started saving for a pension at the age of 23.

### 🚩 Red Flag #2: Taxation Advice

In the UK, all pension income above a certain threshold is subject to income tax.

Advising me to forego AVC contributions at the age of 27 in order to avoid taxation nearly four decades later, struck me as absurd and ridiculous.

### Reflecting on My AVC Decision

To cut a long story short, I ignored the financial advisers and took out an AVC.

After 38 years of contributions, the pot grew to over £154,000, ranking as my fifth largest pension pot upon retirement.

Today, this single AVC provides me with a monthly annuity exceeding £800, easily covering 6 months' worth of petrol costs.

Looking back nearly forty years, had I followed the advice and not invested in an AVC, the £154,000 pension pot is something I would never have accumulated.

So, you might ask: What's the moral of professional financial advice?

🚨 **Here's my take:**

✅ Financial advice is 'reasonable guidance'—it's not mandatory.

✅ The final decision was always mine—it's my money after all.

**Re-evaluating the Role of Financial Advice**

The above real-life examples do not in any way invalidate my original position—that consulting a certified financial adviser is hugely valuable for building wealth especially in retirement and for high performance pension planning. However, they do challenge us to see financial advice differently.

# Chapter

# 3 Pensions Overview and Basics

The Beginning Is The Most Important Part of The Journey

## Buyer Beware. Bad Pension Lasts A Lifetime

Navigating the pension system can seem daunting, but it is a crucial step towards financial independence in retirement. By developing a basic yet knowledgeable understanding of the various types of pensions—state, workplace, and private—an individual can make informed investment decisions that align with their retirement goals. Each pension type offers unique benefits and challenges, and grasping these nuances is essential because doing so helps to maximize your retirement strategy and financial security post-retirement.

For many pension savers, our retirement years are likely to be the most vulnerable and least financially secure period of our lives. This is not only because we face a greater risk of poor health but also due to a potential decline in our standard of living and, in the worst case—poverty. A significant fall in income compared to our pre-retirement period—when we were in high paying employment and relatively well-off—can exacerbate these risks. Therefore, failing to plan properly for retirement, whether through insufficient savings, poor investment choices, or a badly planned pension purchase, puts us at a real risk of undermining our financial security.

### What This Book Is About—and What It Isn't

At this point, I want to be absolutely clear about the scope of this book. To begin with, I will outline what this book is not about. Thereafter, I will discuss its focus and, crucially, why I wrote it.

Planning for retirement is one of life's most crucial financial decisions, yet too many people reach their later years unprepared for the complexities of pension wealth building and transitioning from pension saving to pension buying.

Firstly, this book does not claim to offer pensions or financial advice in any way or form. That's not its purpose. What the book is though is a compendium of my personal, lived experience or points of view (POV) over 40 years, on building pension wealth and transitioning (i.e. pension saving-to-pension buying) into retirement, with a plan built for success and financial security.

### The Purpose Of The Book

This book was written to fill specific knowledge gaps around pension wealth and pension buying. It is an informational guide designed to help individuals successfully navigate the transition from saving for retirement to purchasing a pension—preferably with the substantial pension wealth they've built up.

📌 **What This Book Is:**

✅ An inside track and insight into how I built my pension wealth over 40 years on a salary, starting in my 20s.

✅ A practical, experience-driven roadmap covering the full pension lifecycle, from savings, to taking financial advice and planning for retirement—including readymade template forms to assist with pension purchase.

✅ A step-by-step guide to understanding the crucial difference between pension saving *vs.* pension buying, tax implications, the relevant legislations in simplified and detailed examples of information required for pension purchase.

✅ A hands-on resource and real-world examples of how to prevent pension fraud, avoid scams and seek compensation for delayed pension income, including how to get the best out of the Office of the Pension Ombudsman.

✅A hands-on-guide for getting help with the cost-of-living crisis and critically, hard lessons learnt over 40 years of saving for pension wealth in retirement.

Unlike traditional pension advisory or investment books, this book provides straightforward, jargon-free explanations, equipping readers with the clarity, confidence, and practical knowledge required to make informed choices.

📌 **What The Book Isn't About**

❌ It is not a theoretical work filled with abstract financial advice and theory.

❌ It does not offer financial advice—instead, it encourages readers to reflect on my personal case study and seek professional advice.

❌ It's not an idealistic, one-size-fits-all solution but rather a customizable framework tailored to real-life scenarios—from my own personal experience.

Firstly, by the end of this book, readers will gain practical insights into how I built my pension wealth, pension purchase strategies and transitioned from pension saving to pension purchase/drawdown, ensuring they step into retirement securely, thoughtfully and with confidence—because a bad pension lasts a lifetime—consequently, retirement shouldn't be planned not left to chance.

Secondly, if you're in your 20s, 30s and possibly in your early 40s, you might be interested in how I began growing my pension starting in my 20s. I used a combination of savings, age related salary targets, boosting my pension with annual performance bonus, stock index investments, and literally free money in the form of mandatory employer contributions. The last point was rather important because the higher my salary was the more money I saved into my pension and the higher were my employer contributions.

Furthermore, the book offers practical, straightforward insights and a Code of doctrines, which I developed and used to boost my pension wealth from my 20s, right the way through to my 60s. These strategies were based on six workplace related doctrines that I followed religiously to maximize my earnings, and by so doing, increased my pension savings at no additional cost to me. The doctrines which included starting pension savings early, were simple, actionable blueprints that anyone could emulate which are covered in great detail later on.

Likewise, if you're in your 40s, or early 50s, while it's true the golden pension boat has left the port, it might still be visible even though it's fast approaching the horizon. Yet, with great luck and a favourable wind at your back, it might still be possible to catch the boat before it disappears over the horizon.

That said, for any individual in that age bracket reading this book, I strongly suggest they consult a qualified pensions adviser at their earliest opportunity—like today!

However, if, like me, you are in your 60s, this book is neither about how to save for a pension at your age nor how to pull off eye watering growth on pension investments over a relatively short period of time, and while one must never say never, that kind of investment promise is for scammers, fraudsters and the Marines.

But all is not lost, individuals in their 60s will find the book extremely useful as a hands-on-guide on U.K. pensions purchasing and the application process involved.

The book also includes real-life templates to help individuals successfully navigate annuities purchase, enter income drawdown, and access invaluable information on the Ombudsman and information about available help with the cost-of-living crisis.

**Why Starting Early Matters: Power of Compound Interests**

Without confusing matters with overly complex investment jargon, the key to pension savings—unlike pension purchasing—is contributing to a pension scheme from early adulthood. The advantages of starting early are numerous, but the most important lies in earning returns on initial savings, then earning returns on those returns, which are compounded over time.

And—without meaning to teach my grandmother how to suck eggs—this is called the power of compound interest! Who knows?

With favourable market conditions over several decades, those early pension savings and compound interests could grow into a substantial pension pot. Even modest, regular contributions can accumulate exponentially, creating a considerable financial cushion for retirement.

Thus, the key to pension wealth is timing, constancy, consistency, longevity and luck—that is; regular contributions made over time into a pension pot, allowing time to work its magic.

**Pension 101 — The Pension Lifecycle**

The pension lifecycle consists of three sequential but logical stages that all pension schemes or savers must complete before reaching maturity. If any of these stages are incomplete, a pension scheme might not yield the desired outcome. In the early part of the cycle, contributions form the foundation of a pension and are vital for building a substantial pot.

**1. Contributions**

✅ In the early part of the cycle, contributions form the foundation of a pension and are vital for building a substantial pot.

✅ Regular payments and savings made into pension pots by individuals and their employers in the case of workplace pension.

✅ Includes public sector employees, who benefit from Defined Benefit schemes, even though their employer funds the scheme.

**2. Investments**

✅ Pension funds are invested in stocks, bonds, commercial properties, mutual funds, and other financial instruments.

✅ These investments grow over time, significantly impacting the size of the pension pot.

✅ Although not completely embargoed, however, investments in domestic properties may be precluded by law and by some pension schemes.

**3. Payout**

✅ On reaching retirement, accumulated pension savings can be accessed via:

- Tax-free lump sums
- Taxed lump-sum withdrawals
- Annuities

- Drawdown plans
- Combination of the above options

**The Different Types of Pension Income**

**1. Pension Pot**

✅ The total sum of money accumulated under a pension scheme for retirement.

✅ Building a substantial pension pot is essential for financial security in old age.

**2. Annuities**

✅ Provides a predictable, monthly income stream, similar to employment wages or monthly salaries.

✅ Because annuities offer regular, guaranteed payments, they help with budgeting and financial planning.

✅ Pensioners can choose:

- Fixed-term annuities (*paid over a set number of years*).
- Lifetime annuities (*payments continue for the whole of life*).

🚨 Key consideration: While annuities offer security, they may provide lower returns when compared to investment-based options.

**3.0 Income Drawdown**

Income drawdown gives a retiree full control over their pension pot, allowing them to withdraw funds as needed while keeping the remainder invested. This option offers flexibility and the potential for higher returns if investments perform well.

However, the optimism surrounding higher returns must be balanced against the risks of market volatility and geopolitical events.

A good, cautionary case in point was America's recent tariff trade war of April 2, 2025; commonly referred to as 'Liberation Day' in Republicans. Within weeks of Trump's announcement, stock markets globally lost an estimated U.S. $5.8 trillion (S&P 500 companies). Now, any heavily stock invested drawdown account during America's tariff war period, could have taken a substantial financial hit as a result. Consequently, entering drawdown requires careful consideration, agility, management—and, dare I say, some luck—to ensure that a pensioner does not outlive their savings.

Suffice it to say that at no point during my retirement planning did I consider drawdown income as my sole and only option.

### 4.0 Tax-Free Lump Sums

Taking a tax-free lump sum provides immediate access to a portion of a person's pension pot, which can be used to cover significant unplanned expenses or serve as a financial safety net.

In the UK, the current maximum tax-free lump sum is 25% across all pension pots belonging to a pension saver. Tax is payable on the remaining balance, as it's treated as income by HMRC.

Furthermore, lump sums must be withdrawn in accordance with pension scheme rules and current legislation to avoid significant tax penalties. Because of this—and other financial considerations—it is essential that pensioners carefully plan how they intend to use their lump sum withdrawals to prevent premature depletion of their pension pot.

### 5.0 Combination Pension Pots

A pensioner can mix and match the above withdrawal options to suit their needs, financial plans, and lifestyle.

## Avoiding Common Pension Pitfalls

### 1.0 Age Requirements

Understanding the age at which a pension saver can legally access their pension without incurring severe tax penalties is vital.

- Typically, a pensioner can begin withdrawing funds from their pension pot at age 55.
- Meanwhile, the pension access age limit will rise to 57 from April 2028.
- During an individual's retirement planning phase, it's good practice to check the rules that apply to their pension, as these can vary widely.
- 🚨**CAUTION**:-

  Accessing pension funds early may result in reduced benefits, so timing withdrawals (*lump sum, drawdown, or annuities*) is key to maximizing financial security in retirement.

### 2.0 Fees and Charges

Pensions often come with various administrative fees and management charges that have the potential to erode savings over time.

🚨 **To mitigate high fees, it's crucial to:**

- Stay informed about management fees, transaction costs, and hidden charges associated with pension schemes.
- Regularly review pension plans to assess fees and consider switching to lower-cost schemes if necessary.

Throughout my pension savings years, I frequently (i.e. annually) reviewed my scheme's fee structure with the intention of switching to lower-cost alternatives if needed. Minimizing pension administration fees ensures that more of the savings contributed to growing my pension pot rather than paying unnecessary, excessive fees.

**3.0 Early Withdrawal Penalties**

The timing for legally withdrawing funds from pension savings without incurring substantial tax penalties is governed by current legislation.

- Withdrawing pension funds before reaching the minimum retirement age can result in significant penalties and additional taxes.
- Early withdrawals not only reduce the overall retirement savings but might also trigger extra management charges.

Clearly then, it is crucial that pension savers plan ahead to ensure they access pension funds judiciously, avoiding unnecessary costs while maximizing retirement security and investment growth.

🚨 In certain special circumstances, a pension saver might be able to access pension savings earlier than age 55 (or 57 from April 2028).

These circumstances typically include cases in which the pensioner:

- Becomes mentally or physically incapable of continuing employment.
- Has completely stopped working altogether due to severe health conditions.

**The Three Main Pension Types**

Navigating the pension system can seem daunting, but it's a crucial step toward financial security and independence in retirement.

By taking the time to understand the various pension types—state, workplace, and private—it becomes easier to make informed decisions aligned with retirement aspirations and goals. Each type offers unique benefits and challenges, and understanding these nuances is vital for optimizing retirement choices.

Generally, three primary types of pension schemes dominate in Britain and other mature pension markets, including Canada, the EU, New Zealand, Australia, and the United States.

While various pension types exist—such as Stakeholder pensions or Additional Voluntary Contributions (AVC)—these are essentially variations of Defined Benefit (DB) and Defined Contribution (DC) pensions, with legislative nuances regarding permitted investment types, fees, and other factors. Therefore, the three, common pension scheme types are as follows:-

- (a) - Workplace Pensions
    - Defined Benefit Pension
    - Defined Contribution Pension
- (b) - UK State Pensions
- (c) - Self-Invested Personal Pensions (SIPP)

## 1.0 Workplace Pensions

Workplace pensions are provided by employers under legal obligations set by the Pensions Act 2008. Under this legislation, all UK employers must enrol eligible staff into a pension scheme and contribute to it—a process known as automatic enrolment.

Workplace pensions exist in two forms: Defined Benefit **(DB)** and Defined Contribution **(DC)** schemes.

### 1.1 Defined Benefit Pensions

A Defined Benefit (DB) pension is a retirement plan in which employers guarantee a specific pension income upon retirement.

The benefit amount is determined by a formula based on average salary, years of service with the employer, and an internal multiplier (e.g. 1-2% per year of service).

For example, if an individual has a DB pension with 30 years of service with the same employer, a 2% multiplier rate, and a final/average salary of £60,000, they will receive £36,000 per year, guaranteed for life. This was calculated as follows: [30 years' service X 0.02 (2%) X £60,000 = £36,000].

DB pensions are funded solely by employer contributions, meaning all financial risks and responsibilities rests with the employer.

Employers must ensure sufficient funds are available to meet future obligations. If market performance declines or lifespans increase, the employer must contribute additional funds to cover obligations.

Defined Benefits are typically paid as a lifetime annuity, beginning at a designated retirement age (e.g. 65).

Employees may need to meet a minimum service period (e.g. five years) to qualify for full benefits, and early departures from an employer may result in reduced payouts.

### 1.1.1 Benefits and Drawbacks of DB Pensions

**For Employees:**

✅ Predictable, lifelong income unaffected by market volatility.

✅ Often includes cost-of-living adjustments (COLA) to combat inflation.

✅ If an employer is insolvent and the pension scheme lacks sufficient assets, the Pension Protection Fund (PPF) steps in to ensure payments.

❌ Less portable—leaving an employer early may result in forfeited benefits.

❌ Pension stability depends on employer financial health

**For Employers:**

✅ Enhances employee loyalty and retention.

❌ High costs, complexity, and regulatory burden.

❌ Requires significant financial resources.

❌ Employer assumes liability for pension shortfalls due to market downturns or longevity risk.

In the private sector, adoption of DB pensions has declined sharply over the past 20-30 years, as employers increasingly shift pension investment risks onto employees through Defined Contribution (DC) schemes.

Although, in the public sector (teachers, civil servants, firefighters, police officers, military personnel, and NHS employees), DB pensions remain widely used to attract and retain staff.

### 1.2 Defined Contribution Pensions

A Defined Contribution (DC) pension differs significantly from DB pensions because contributions come from both the employer and the employee and are invested in a pension pot. The final pension value depends on the performance of these investments, making DC pensions more flexible but riskier for employees compared to DB schemes.

Unlike DB pensions, DC plans are entirely dependent on market performance, meaning they do not guarantee a specific payout. Employees assume investment risk, which could lead to substantial pension growth—but could also result in lower-than-expected retirement funds if markets perform poorly.

Both the employee and employer contribute to a Defined Contribution (DC) scheme. By law, employers must contribute a minimum of 3% of the employee's qualifying earnings toward their workplace pension, although they may contribute more. Speaking from personal experience, during the last 20 years of my professional career before retirement, many of my past employers matched my contribution which was typically 15% of my salary.

The total minimum contribution for employees is 8% of qualifying earnings. There's no set maximum for employee workplace pension contributions, but the total contributions—including those from the employee, employer, and any tax relief—may not exceed the annual allowance, which is £60,000 for the 2025/26 tax year. This limit applies to all pension savings, including workplace and personal pensions such as Self-Invested Personal Pensions (SIPPs).

However, unlike Defined Benefit (DB) pensions, the risk in DC pensions rests solely with the employee, as investment gains or losses directly impact the size of the pot. Consequently, poor market performance or poor investment choices can reduce the pot's value upon retirement.

### 1.2.1 Benefits & Drawbacks of Defined Contribution Pensions

**For Employees**

✅ Control – Employees choose their investments (e.g. stocks, bonds, etc).

✅ Portability – Pension savings can be transferred when changing jobs.

✅ Transparency – Employees can track balances and growth in real time.

✅ Flexible Withdrawal Options – Funds can be withdrawn as a lump sum, annuity, or periodic payments (income drawdown).

❌ Market Risk – Retirement income depends on investment performance.

❌ Longevity Risk – For individuals taking drawdown income, savings may run out if withdrawals exceed investment growth.

**For Employers**

✅ Cost Predictability – Contributions are fixed (no long-term liabilities).

✅ Simpler Administration – No complex actuarial calculations.

❌ Retention Challenges – Employees may leave if employer contributions are on the low side.

DC pension plans shift retirement risk from employers to employees, providing flexibility and portability but requiring active involvement of employees in the management of investments and longevity risks. DC schemes dominate modern retirement planning, particularly in the private sector, making proactive financial literacy and management essential for successful retirement outcomes.

DC pensions are widely used across many Anglophone nations, although they're known by different names as the ensuing list shows:

- **United Kingdom** – Personal Pension Plans
- **United States** – 401(k) Plans
- **New Zealand** – KiwiSaver
- **Canada** – RRSP (Registered Retirement Savings Plan)
- **Australia** – Superannuation

## 2.0 UK State Pensions

The UK State Pension provides only a basic income in retirement. Compared to the UK's 2025 minimum wage of £12.21/hour, the new weekly State Pension of £230.25 (tax year 2025/2026) is equivalent to around £6.14/hour. This amount is significantly lower than the current (2024/2025) minimum wage!

For pensioners on the older, basic State Pension, the situation is far worse. The full amount of £176.45 per week is equivalent to £4.70/hour! In fact, the U.K. state pension remains one of the lowest state pensions among European countries with comparable living standards.

To ensure financial security in retirement, it is essential to combine the State Pension with private pensions (workplace or personal) and other savings. Even before the cost-of-living crisis, the UK State Pension provided only a safety net, but was rarely sufficient for a comfortable retirement.

**How the UK State Pension Works**

The UK State Pension is a regular payment made every four weeks by the Department for Work and Pensions (DWP) to qualifying U.K. pensioners.

Individuals must have at least 10 years of National Insurance (NI) contributions to qualify and must have reached the eligible retirement age in force at the time.

## 2.1 Key Features of the UK State Pension

## 2.2 Types of State Pension:

- New State Pension – For those who reached retirement age on or after April 6, 2016.
- Basic State Pension – For those who reached retirement age before April 6, 2016.

## 2.3 Eligibility

- Minimum 10 qualifying years of National Insurance (NI) contributions are required for any pension payment.
- To receive the full New State Pension, individuals currently need 35 qualifying years (though transitional rules may apply).

## 2.4 State Pension Amount (2024-2025)

- New State Pension: £221.20 per week
- Basic State Pension: Up to £169.50 per week (for those who retired earlier)

## 2.5 State Pension Age:

- Currently 66 for both men and women.
- Rising to 67 by 2028 and 68 by 2046 or earlier.

## 2.6 How to Claim the State Pension

- The State Pension is not automatically awarded—qualifying individuals must apply to claim it. 🔗https://www.gov.uk/get-state-pension Apply for UK State Pension
- Eligible claimants may receive an invitation from the DWP to apply.
- If an eligible claimant has reached State Pension age but has not received an invitation, they can apply via the Apply using the link above.

## 2.7 How NI Contributions Affect The State Pension:

- **Paid NI Contributions** – Contributions made through employment, self-employment, or voluntary payments count towards qualifying years.
- **Gaps in NI Record** – Missing years can be topped up to increase the state pension upon reaching State Pension age. Although the opportunity to 'top-up' is restricted to specific calendar windows which are obtainable directly from HMRC📞0300 200 3500 —📞Textphone 0300 200 3519. The best time to call are Wednesday late morning and mid-afternoon on weekdays.

## 2.8 Deferring Your State Pension

Individuals may choose to delay claiming their State Pension, resulting in an increase in weekly payments.

- The weekly amount increases by circa 1% for every nine weeks deferred
- This is equivalent to an annual uplift of 5.8%.

## 2.9 Receiving the UK State Pension While Living Abroad

British pensioners can still receive their UK State Pension if they move abroad.

- Pension claims from overseas residents must be made through the International Pension Centre:
  - Phone: 📞+44 (0) 191 218 7777
  - Web: 🔗 https://www.gov.uk/international-pension-centre
- Pensioners can receive payments into a UK bank account—regardless of where they live.
- Pensioners may also opt to receive payments into a local bank account in their country of residence.

### 2.9.1 Additional Considerations for Overseas Pension

- If opting for a local overseas bank account, payments will be made in the local currency, meaning amounts may fluctuate due to exchange rates.
- UK State Pensions may be frozen (i.e., not increased yearly) in certain countries without reciprocal agreements.

## 2.10 Common Issues with the UK State Pension

❌ Inadequate Income – The State Pension alone is rarely sufficient for retirement; private pensions or other savings may be needed.

❌ Rising State Pension Age – Future increases may affect younger workers.

❌ Gender & Historical Gaps – Some older women receive lower pensions due to past National Insurance contribution rules.

As a comparison exercise, you'll find below a concise overview of state pensions in Western Anglophone countries comprising Australia, Canada, Eire, New Zealand and the United States.

In general terms each country has its variant or flavour of the U.K. State Pension qualification age(s), however, that's where the common grounds on pensions end.

Specifically, each state has unique pension funding structures or formulas, legislation, and regulations that balance tax-funded benefits with individual contributions.

**Australia**

- **System Name:** Superannuation
- **Eligibility:** Based on age (67+), residency, and income/assets test.
- **Funding:** Means-tested; funded through general taxation, not individual contributions.
- **Payment Amount:** Varies based on income/assets; maximum rate for singles is around AUD 1,064 per fortnight.
- **Superannuation:** Mandatory employer contributions (Superannuation Guarantee) supplement retirement income.
- **Indexation:** Adjusted biannually based on inflation and wages.

**Canada**

- **System Name:** Canada Pension Plan (CPP) & Old Age Security (OAS)
- **Eligibility:** CPP requires contributions during working

years; OAS is residency-based (age 65+).

- **Funding:** CPP is funded by payroll contributions; OAS is tax-funded.
- **Payment Amount:** CPP depends on earnings history; OAS provides a basic pension amount (CAD $713/month).
- **Additional Benefits:** Guaranteed Income Supplement (GIS) for low-income retirees.
- **Indexation:** Adjusted quarterly for inflation.

**New Zealand**

- **System Name:** New Zealand Superannuation (NZ Super)
- **Eligibility:** Residency-based (age 65+); no income or asset test.
- **Funding:** Tax-funded; no mandatory contributions.
- **Payment Amount:** Flat-rate pension (NZD $994.00-$1076.84/fortnight for singles and NZD $1,598.42/fortnight for qualifying couples).
- **KiwiSaver:** Voluntary retirement savings scheme with employer and government contributions.
- **Indexation:** Adjusted annually based on inflation and wages.

**Ireland (Eire)**

- **System Name:** State Pension (Contributory & Non-Contributory)
- **Eligibility:** Contributory pension requires PRSI contributions (age 66); non-contributory is means-tested.
- **Funding:** Contributory pension funded by payroll taxes; non-contributory is tax-funded.
- **Payment Amount:** Contributory pension (EUR €277/week); non-contributory varies based on income.
- **Additional Benefits:** Household benefits package, fuel allowance, and free travel scheme.
- **Indexation:** Adjusted periodically by government policy.

**United States of America**

- **System Name**: Social Security Retirement Benefits
- **Eligibility:** Based on work history and Social Security credits (age 66-67); minimum 40 credits, typically 10 years of work.
- **Funding:** Payroll taxes (FICA); employer and employee contributions.
- **Payment Amount:** Depends on earnings history; average pension (USD $1,900/month).

- **Additional Benefits:** Supplemental Security Income (SSI) for low-income retirees.
- **Indexation:** Adjusted annually based on inflation (Cost-of-Living Adjustment - COLA).

### 3.0 Self-Invested Personal Pension (SIPP)

A Self-Invested Personal Pension (SIPP) is a form of Defined Contribution (DC) pension taken out and managed by an individual. By comparison, a Workplace defined contribution scheme is created by an employer and managed by a pension provider on the employer's behalf.

A SIPP is tax-efficient, as contributions attract tax relief based on the highest tax band paid by the contributor. It also offers high flexibility, but—like all DC pensions—the SIPP owner carries all investment risks.

A SIPP is not constrained by the investment limitations placed on Workplace or Stakeholder pensions, which have restricted investment choices. A stakeholder pension is simpler but more regulated, with limited investment options and capped charges (typically around 1% of the pot's value).

Recently, low-cost SIPPs have become increasingly available, although fees can erode returns over time. This makes management fees and cost comparisons critical for the pension holder.

SIPPs can be particularly beneficial for self-employed individuals and directors of limited companies, as contributions can be made from company profits, reducing taxable income and potentially lowering corporation tax. Interestingly, this flexibility allows self-employed individuals to contribute as both employer and employee, leading to enhanced contributions and substantial tax savings.

### 3.1 Eligibility and Withdrawal Age

A SIPP can be set up by any UK individual aged between 18 and 75. When the regulatory minimum age is reached—currently 55 years old—the pension holder may begin drawing funds from the SIPP.

However, from April 2028, the minimum age for crystallizing or withdrawing SIPP pensions will increase from 55 to 57. This change reflects increasing life expectancy in the UK and will apply to most individuals born after April 6, 1971.

### 3.2 Tax Advantages of SIPPs

✅ Tax Relief on Contributions

- Basic-rate taxpayers receive a 20% top-up from the government (*e.g. an £80 contribution becomes £100*).

- Higher-rate taxpayers can claim additional relief via self-assessment.

✅ **Tax-Free Growth**

- Investments grow free of UK capital gains and income tax.

✅ **Tax-Free Lump Sum**

- Up to 25% of the pension pot can be withdrawn tax-free at retirement.

### 3.3 Contribution Limits

- **Annual Allowance:** Up to £60,000 (2023/24) or 100% of earnings, whichever is lower.
- **Non-Earners:** Can contribute £2,880 annually, topped up to £3,600 with tax relief.
- **Carry-Forward Rule:** Unused allowances from the past three years can be utilized.

### 3.4 Risks and Considerations

❌ Investment Risk: Market volatility means returns are not guaranteed, and losses are possible.

❌ Access Restrictions: Funds are locked until age 55 (*rising to 57 from 2028*).

❌ Complexity: Managing a SIPP requires financial literacy or professional advice, especially for complex assets like commercial property.

**3.5 For U.S. citizens or Green Card holders resident in the UK**

✅ **Reporting Requirements:**

- SIPPs are classified as foreign trusts, requiring annual filing of IRS Forms 3520 and 3520-A.
- Missing filing deadlines may incur penalties up to $10,000.

✅ **Tax Treatment**

- Under the U.S.-UK tax treaty, SIPPs qualify as tax-deferred pensions, meaning growth remains untaxed until withdrawal.
- However, the 25% tax-free lump sum allowance is not recognized by the IRS—meaning it does not apply to Green Card holders.

✅ **PFIC Concerns**

- Investments in foreign mutual funds (*e.g., ETFs*) may trigger Passive Foreign Investment Company (PFIC) reporting.

However, SIPPs under the U.S.-UK tax treaties often simplify this process.

# Chapter

# 4 Legal Digest - Key Pension Laws In Focus

Laws Are Felt Only When An Individual Comes Into Contact With Them

## Pension Laws And Regulations - Why You Should Care

Professional financial advisers and the media frequently remind us how complex pension laws, legislation and regulations are—and indeed they're right to do so. Although, regardless of this view, it does not mean individuals saving for a pension should abdicate total responsibility for understanding the basic tenets of pension laws, that they might inadvertently violate due to ignorance or lack of professional financial advice. After all, whether a person likes it or not, in a similar fashion to road traffic laws and regulations, for better or for worse, pension regulations can impact their life.

While any comparison runs the risk of going too far, nonetheless, a useful parallel is the Road Traffic Act 1988, which covers the Highway Code, driving tests and issuance of road driving licence. While most drivers on UK roads today are unlikely to be intimately familiar with the nuts and bolts of the 1988 Act, all British drivers are required to master the Highway Code and pass a driving test before being allowed on the road.

Similarly, while pension scheme members are not expected to master the Pensions Act 2014, ideally, they should have a basic understanding of pension laws—just as they do with the Highway Code. This was the approach I took heading into retirement. I purposely set out to acquire a working knowledge of relevant pension laws, particularly those relating to pension purchase applications—a process I knew very little about. My grasp of the relevant legislation relating to pensions, proved invaluable when I successfully lodged two five-figures claims against two pension providers for unreasonable delays in the start of my annuity payments.

### The Impact of Pension Regulation on UK Pension Savers

Depending on one's perception or perspective, UK pension savers experience a highly regulated pension industry—which is both a blessing and a curse. On the one hand, regulations provide consumer protection and security. On the other hand, they create a complex environment that can be challenging to navigate.

The specifics of this complexity lie beyond the scope of this book but understanding some regulations either at a basic or guideline level is helpful, as they directly impact the structure and operation of all pension schemes, including workplace pensions, private pensions, and consumer protections.

For example, as of 2025, the latest UK pension legislation introduced changes to the Lifetime Allowance (LTA), lump sum allowances, and the state pension age. These updates demonstrate why pension savers must remain informed about key pension laws—because doing so can make all the difference to securing financial stability in retirement. Beyond the Pensions Act 2014, the current landscape of U.K. pension laws and regulations are constantly shaped by the two key mechanisms discussed below:

### Legislative Updates

Pension laws and regulations are dynamic legal mechanisms subject to change. Staying informed about these updates is vital for effective retirement planning, as legislative changes can affect various pension parameters, including contribution limits, tax benefits, and withdrawal rules. By keeping up to date with these changes, individuals can modify their pension plans to maximize tax benefits and avoid potential financial pitfalls.

### Policy Changes

Government policies related to pensions can significantly impact retirement plans. For example, changes in the age at which pensions can be accessed, or legislative adjustments to the state pension age and other entitlements, can alter retirement timelines.

Understanding these policy changes allows individuals to plan effectively, ensuring they take full advantage of available benefits while avoiding drawbacks.

**The Pensions Regulator**

The Pensions Regulator (TPR) Telephone: 📞0345 600 1011 is the primary regulator of work-based pensions in the UK, and its codes of practice, although not legislation, are highly influential. U.K's Finance Acts are updated annually, and pensions tax rules often evolve through these (e.g. changes to Annual Allowance or tapered allowances).

What follows below is a summary of the Top Ten U.K. laws and regulations, which are in my experience, arguably the most influential and relevant to pension savers. The laws and regulations cover Acts of Parliament, regulations, case laws and regulatory guidelines. These laws apply to private pensions and occupational schemes alike. As far as it's possible to do so, I have summarised the essence of the regulations and highlighted the motivation behind each one.

**Top 10 Most Influential UK Pension and Tax Laws**

As I approached retirement planning back in 2020, I investigated online (where else?) the pension laws that were most likely to impact my pension pots when I came to retire. Similarly to my Road Traffic analogy above, I stuck to the key provisions of each legislation as it affected me, without getting lost in the weeds.

In this context, here's a carefully curated list of the Top 10 most influential UK pension and tax laws since 1990—each a landmark piece of legislation that shaped Britain's pension industry. These laws transformed the UK's pension sector from State Pension reforms to auto-enrolment, taxation rules, and consumer protection measures. For any individual planning to retire, understanding the basic provisions of these laws and regulations is useful, in case they wish to take further advice on them.

### 1. Pensions Act 199: The Post-Maxwell Wake-Up Call

The collapse of Robert Maxwell's pension empire sent a seismic shock through the UK pension system, exposing vulnerabilities in scheme governance. Maxwell literally screwed over thousands of British workers whose pensions funded his lavish lifestyle, before his apparent suicide. The Pensions Act 1995 was U.K.'s urgent response, ensuring greater oversight and security for occupational pensions.

Despite the 1995 Act, in 2016, The British Home Stores (BHS) pension scandal followed the collapse of BHS, resulting in a pension deficit of over £570 million with 19,000 employees left in the lurch! This called into question the robustness of that law. Parliament was compelled to look at further legal means of reigning in rogue bosses, resulting in the 2021 Pension Schemes Act. This law was a watershed in Pension laws by giving more powers to the TPR.

📌 **Key Provisions**

✅ Introduced minimum funding requirements to protect pension assets.

✅ Established Pensions Regulator (then OPRA) to oversee pensions schemes.

✅ Mandated compulsory member protection measures, including pension trustees' responsibilities.

**2. Pension Schemes Act 2021: Pension Regulator Power Grab**

Following other high-profile pension failures post The Daily Mirror's Robert Maxwell, the previously mentioned BHS pension scandal by Philip Green undoubtedly lit the blue touch paper for this law. The employer, Trustees of the scheme and the regulator faced heavy criticism in the press and in parliament.

The Pension Schemes Act 2021 equipped The Pensions Regulator (TPR) with stronger enforcement powers. The Act also introduced significant changes for trustees, including new funding and investment strategy requirements. Overall, the Act imposed greater accountability for scheme trustees and employers.

📌 **Key Provisions**

✅ Introduced new criminal offences for reckless mismanagement of pensions.

✅ Increased corporate accountability for pension funding.

✅ Strengthened pension transfer protections for consumers.

### 3. Finance Act 2004: The Simplifier That Changed Everything

Before 2004, UK pension taxation was a tangled web and frankly a 'fine mess', to coin a phrase by Stan Laurel & Oliver Hardy of the Laurel & Hardy comedy show.

The Finance Act 2004 revolutionized the UK tax system, consolidating several tax laws including those affecting pensions into a single framework. It also introduced the Lifetime Allowance (LTA), and paved the way for flexible pensions.

📌 **Key Provisions**

✅ Introduced the Lifetime Allowance (LTA), capping tax-free pension savings.

✅ Established pension tax relief limits, ensuring consistency across schemes.

✅ Allowed greater flexibility in pension withdrawals.

**4. Pensions Act 2007: Redefining the State Pension**

By the 2000s, Britain's State Pension system was antiquated and in urgent need of reform because it was for the most part skewed in favour of men and the qualifying criteria was burdensome. The Pensions Act 2007 modernized eligibility rules, making the system more inclusive for women, carers and other non-earners.

📌 **Key Provisions**

✅ Reduced State Pension qualifying years from 44 (men) / 39 (women) to 30.

✅ Allowed carers and lower-income workers to qualify more easily.

✅ Set the groundwork for future State Pension increases.

**5. Pensions Act 2008: The Auto-Enrolment Revolution**

This was the 'Great Leap Forward' in pension laws that brought millions of British workers in from the cold, and into the fold.

Prior to this Act, millions of workers were missing out on pensions, therefore, the government took decisive action.

The Pensions Act 2008 introduced auto-enrolment, ensuring that employers actively enrolled eligible workers into pension schemes.

📌 **Key Provisions**

✅ Made auto-enrolment mandatory for eligible employees.

✅ Required minimum employer contributions.

✅ Established the National Employment Savings Trust (NEST) to manage auto-enrolment.

**6. Finance Act 2011: Raising the Stakes on Tax Relief**

This was Britain's Benjamin Franklin moment a la *'Nothing is certain except death and taxes'.* With pension tax relief under scrutiny, the Finance Act 2011 introduced significant restrictions, limiting the Annual Savings Allowance and tightening the rules on high earners' pension tax advantages.

📌 **Key Provisions**

✅ Reduced the Annual Allowance from £255,000 to £50,000.

✅ Cut the Lifetime Allowance from £1.8 million to £1.5 million.

✅ Introduced stricter pension tax relief measures to curb excessive claims.

### 7. Pensions Act 2014: A New Age for Retirement

The 2014 Pensions Act channelled John Dryden's ''Tis well an old age is out, And time to begin a new'! This landmark Act reshaped the State Pension, introducing the new flat-rate State Pension and abolishing the Second State Pension (S2P). It simplified retirement forecasts and ensured greater predictability for pensioners.

📌 **Key Provisions**

✅ Created the new flat-rate State Pension, replacing S2P.

✅ Increased State Pension age in line with longevity trends

✅ Improved protections for defined benefit scheme members.

### 8. Taxation of Pensions Act 2014: The Freedom Revolution

The Taxation of Pensions Act 2014 delivered pension freedom, giving pension savers unprecedented control over their pension savings. This was the law that created the myth of Ferrari driving retirees, if only it was true! Suddenly, individuals could withdraw their pensions flexibly, rather than purchasing an annuity.

📌 **Key Provisions**

✅ Allowed full pension pot withdrawals from age 55.

✅ Removed the requirement to buy an annuity.

✅ Implemented flexible drawdown options with new tax rules.

### 9. Pension Schemes Act 2017: Cracking Down on Scams

With the 2017 Act, ' The Empire struck back' against proliferating pension scams and frauds. Pension fraud was on the rise, with scammers exploiting transfer loopholes.

The Pension Schemes Act 2017 introduced new safeguards, making it harder to move pensions into fraudulent schemes. The Act also created a new regulatory framework for Master Trusts that provide a pension solution for employers wanting a trust-based scheme, without the cost and management overheads.

📌 **Key Provisions**

✅ Strengthened pension transfer scrutiny, blocking suspicious schemes.

✅ Gave regulators more power to intervene in fraudulent activity.

✅ Required greater transparency and reporting for pension funds.

### 10. Finance Act 2023: Abolishing the Lifetime Allowance

The jury is still out whether or not the political division over LTA abolition has left future pension tax rules in something of a quandary. The Finance Act 2023 was one of the most controversial pension tax reforms in decades because it abolished the Lifetime allowance, allowing individuals to save more without crushing tax penalties.

This Act is an antidote to the Finance Act 2011.

📌 **Key Provisions:**

✅ Eliminated the £1,073,100 (£1.07m) Lifetime Allowance cap.

✅ Removed previous tax charges on excess pension savings.

✅ Restructured pension lump sum taxation rules.

**Top 20 Most Influential Pensions Legislation & Regulations**

Above, I've provided a synopsis of my Top 10 legislations and legal guidelines. Now, I will give a summary of the Top 20 legislations and quasi-legislation that has shaped U.K pensions.

My review of the Top 20 legislation is a high-level summary in easily digestible format covering the scope and the year of enactment.

I compiled most of this list back in 2020 and used it in my discussions with FCA regulated financial advisers.

By drawing up a list of pension legislations, it was easy to focus on the narrow aspects of the pension laws that I was interested in. I used it as a 'To-Do-List' to demonstrate to my advisers that I was serious and had done my homework.

**Fig. 7.0 Top 20 Most Influential Pensions Legislation**

| Laws and Regulations | Year | Short Description & Relevance |
|---|---|---|
| Pensions Act | 1995 | Introduced minimum funding requirements, strengthened member protections & created the Occupational Pensions Regulatory Authority (OPRA) |
| Pensions Act | 2004 | Replaced OPRA with The Pensions Regulator (TPR); established the Pension Protection Fund (PPF); introduced scheme funding regime. |
| Pensions Act | 2007 | Increased State Pension Age (SPA) and reformed the basic State Pension to improve fairness. |
| Pensions Act | 2008 | Introduced auto-enrolment duties for employers and the creation of the National Employment Savings Trust (NEST). |

| | | |
|---|---|---|
| Pensions Act | 2004 | Simplified pension tax rules under the "A-Day" reforms of 2006, including the introduction of the Lifetime and Annual Allowances. |
| Pensions Act | 2023 | Removed the Lifetime Allowance charge (to be formally abolished in April 2024), marking a significant shift in pensions tax policy. |
| Social Security Contributions and Benefits Act | 1992 | Governs National Insurance contributions and State Pension entitlement calculations. |
| Income Tax (Earnings and Pensions) Act (ITEPA) | 2003 | Core tax legislation covering pensions and employment income, including employer contributions and benefits. |
| Pension Schemes Act | 1993 | Codified preservation of benefits and revaluation of deferred pensions; contains key provisions on contracting-out. |
| Pension Schemes Act | 2015 | Introduced new types of schemes, including Collective |

| | | |
|---|---|---|
| | | Defined Contribution (CDC) schemes, and allowed for greater scheme design flexibility. |
| Taxation of Pensions Act | 2014 | Enabled pension freedoms from age 55, allowing full withdrawal of defined contribution (DC) pots and flexible access. |
| Occupational and Personal Pension Schemes (Disclosure of Information) Regulations | 2013 | Sets out the information trustees must provide to members. Crucial for transparency. |
| Occupational Pension Schemes (Investment) Regulations | 2005 | Requires trustees to produce a Statement of Investment Principles; includes ESG duties. |
| The Pensions Regulator Code of Practice | Various | Provides guidance on governance, funding, and compliance. Not legislation but quasi-legal influence. |
| Employment Rights Act (relevant sections) | 1996 | Contains provisions protecting pension rights |

| | | |
|---|---|---|
| | | during business transfers (TUPE regulations). |
| Equality Act | 2010 | Prohibits discrimination in pensions on grounds such as age, sex, disability, etc. |
| Freedom and Choice in Pensions (HM Treasury Policy) | 2014 | Policy initiative underlying pension freedoms, facilitating drawdown, lump sum access, etc. |
| State Pension Regulations (New State Pension) | 2016 | Established the flat-rate State Pension for people reaching SPA on/after 6 April 2016. |
| Auto Enrolment Regulations | 2012<br>2017 | Sets staging dates and duties for employers under auto-enrolment; enforced by TPR. |
| Trustee Act | 2000 | Governs trustee powers and duties, especially investment duties relevant to pension scheme trustees. |

### Contacting The Pensions Regulator

The Pensions Regulator is part of the regulatory framework for UK pensions and can be reached as follows:

- Telephone: 📞0345 600 1011
- Email: cande@autoenrol.tpr.gov.uk

**Address:**

Customer Support,

The Pensions Regulator,

Telecom House,

125-135 Preston Road,

Brighton, BN1 6AF,

East Sussex

# Chapter

# 5 Buying A Pension and Decumulation

The Art Is Not In Making Money But Keeping It

## A Big Pot Does Not Auto Translate Into A Large Pension

First off, many people wrongly assume that a pension pot is like the proverbial pot of gold waiting at the end of the rainbow or, less dramatically, akin to a bank account that can be accessed at will from age 55, at anytime, anyplace and anywhere. However, nothing could be further from the truth. Unlike bank accounts—or the imaginary pot of gold at the end of a rainbow—pension pots are highly regulated and come with severe tax penalties if withdrawn without paying heed to the prevailing legislative framework applicable to pensions.

Much of the confusion about access arises from the lack of distinction between saving for a pension while employed and buying one in retirement. As a result, many people approaching retirement wrongly assume they will have swift and unrestricted access to their savings or nest egg. But, as always, truth is stranger than fiction—because accessing pension funds requires following a specific pension purchase application process and observing any applicable legislation constraints. As a further matter, the ease or the difficulty of this process depends entirely on the internal procedures and operational capabilities of each pension provider, which can be confusing, patchy and at times daunting.

### A Large Pot Does Not Automatically Guarantee A Good Pension

Things only become more complicated when an individual realises the nest egg is not the pension, but rather a means to an end, and without good, professional financial advice and personal judgement, a superficially large pension pot, will not automatically translate into the good retirement income anticipated by a pension saver.

Crucially, while a larger pot provides more options in retirement, the actual pension income received depends on how the pension pot was managed or utilized, withdrawn, as well as factors like inflation, fees and investment returns as described below.

The relationship between pension size and income is influenced by several critical factors:

### 1. Income Withdrawal Strategy

A large pot can be frittered away quickly without a disciplined drawdown plan guided by pre-planning and scenario modelling. For example, withdrawing 10% annually could exhaust a £500,000 pot in less than 15 years, notably if market conditions are poor or living costs rise sharply, potentially resulting in the pension saver outliving their savings.

The commonly cited 4% rule suggests withdrawing 4% annually to preserve capital, but even this requires periodic adjustments based on market performance and inflation.

**2. Annuity Rates vs. Investment Returns**

If the assumed £500K pot is used to purchase an annuity, the income is fixed based on prevailing interest rates. Currently, annuity rates vary and are tied to interest rates and life expectancy. According to some UK annuity calculators, a £500,000 pot for a 65-year-old might yield around £30,000 a year—before inflation and taxes.

Alternatively, keeping the pot invested (i.e. drawdown) while taking 4% annually, exposes the retiree to market volatility, longevity risk (outliving the pot), and sequencing risks (taking money out during market downturns).

Ultimately, good income depends on smart asset allocation, market timing, geo-political developments and a dose of luck! Perhaps Napoleon Bonaparte ("Give me a lucky general any day") had a point!

### 3. Taxation

Withdrawals from a pension pot—aside from the 25% tax-free lump sum—are treated by HMRC as income consequently they're subject to income tax.

Unintentionally, a large pot may accidentally push retirees into higher tax brackets, reducing net income.

### 4. Inflation

Without inflation protection, the real value of income can erode over time. At 2% inflation, a £30,000 annual income today could have the purchasing power of just over £20,000 in 20 years.

## Income Modelling and Scenario Planning

Income modelling and scenario planning is not unlike the 'Future History' concept which I described in an earlier chapter.

The concept is as much about forethought and preparation as income modelling and scenario planning are, so that an individual can visualise how different pension purchase strategies, lifestyle choices, and so forth, might shape their life in retirement.

Generally speaking, there are four key criteria or inputs for the modelling and planning activity, which are discussed in full below. I will then use these inputs to build and run a simple income modelling and scenario planning exercise.

📌**INPUT #1: Estimate Retirement Expenses**

Start by outlining your desired annual retirement spending profile to Include:

- **Essential** costs (housing, food, utilities etc)
- **Discretionary** spending (travel, eating out, gifts etc)
- **Unplanned** costs (healthcare, home repairs, car repairs etc)

🚨**Let's say you aim for £35,000 per year in today's money.**

📌**INPUT #2: Adjust for Inflation**

For example, if you plan to retire in 10 years, and the Bank of England estimates average inflation over 10 years at 2.5% annually (i.e. 0.025 x 10 x £35,000) = £8,750, thus making the £35,000 target become about £44,750 (i.e. (£35,000 + £8,750) in real terms!

📌**INPUT #3: Calculate Sustainable Drawdown**

Using the widely touted 4% rule as a starting point or starter for ten: A £44,800 annual income suggests a pension pot of roughly £1.12m.

- But this rule isn't sacred—it assumes a 30-year retirement, steady returns, and moderate inflation. Many planners now prefer a flexible withdrawal approach, adjusting annually based on market performance.

📌**INPUT #4: Total Income Inflow**

Then combine the different income streams to calculate the total annual income.

- State pension (e.g. £11,500/year)
- Annuity from defined benefit schemes (e.g. £11,500/year)
- Drawdown from defined contribution pensions (e.g. £11,500/year)
- Rental income, ISAs, part-time work (e.g. £11,500/year)

🚨**Total Cash Inflow: £46,000 annual income**

📌**Model Scenarios:**

**Run Different Scenarios against projected annual income**

Having modelled your income including drawdown such that you don't outlive your pot; you should then test how your pension income fares under various conditions or scenarios:

- Market downturn early in retirement
- Living 30 vs. 40 years post-retirement
- High inflation periods (e.g. recent cost-of-living crisis is an example)
- Delaying retirement by 2–3 years

## The Complexity of Pension Purchasing

There are several compelling reasons why Stakeholder (workplace and private) purchasing processes are convoluted, but the most significant is the security barriers erected around each pension pot by providers—to guard against fraud and scams.

Another major contributing factor to the complexity of pension purchasing, are the administrative and regulatory overheads that surround pension purchasing.

Thus, while this book provides a thorough analysis of the pension purchasing process and building pension wealth, it also serves as a practical guide on how to successfully navigate the pension buying system.

A planned and predictable approach to transitioning from employment (i.e. pension saving) to retirement (i.e. pension buying) is key. Methodical planning, informed learning, and thorough pensions pre-purchase preparation are essential to minimizing or eliminating delays in receiving the all-important first pension income, whether you're entering drawdown or buying an annuity.

🚨 **Caveat Emptor: Buyer Be Warned!**

**The Irrevocable Nature of Pension Choices**

As I considered my options, modelled my likely scenarios and navigated my pension application process, I concluded that buying a pension after decades of uneventful dull savings, was akin to driving a car with no reverse gear down a narrow, one-way, country lane with angry bulls at my back—with no chance of turning back!

🚨 **Once you make your annuity choice, that's it—you're locked in for life!**

## Decumulation

### Pension Decumulation: What It Is and How to Plan for It

Most retirement advice focuses on *accumulation*—how to build a sizable pot over your working life. But what happens when the monthly paycheques stop and the pension begins? That's what *decumulation* is: the process of turning your savings into a reliable, sustainable income stream during retirement.

Pension decumulation isn't just about drawing money—it's about managing longevity risk (the chance that you might outlive your funds), market volatility, inflation, and personal lifestyle choices. Done well, it transforms a pot of capital into peace of mind. Done poorly, it can result in money running out too soon or living more cautiously than necessary.

Ultimately, the starting point is to work with a professional and regulated financial advisor, to create a budget and spending plan aligned to your lifestyle and expectations, taking into consideration and inputs from the Income modelling and scenario planning analysis that we discussed above.

There are several pathways to decumulation. To drive home this point, I've taken a building block approach by listing below the key components for consideration and action at the appropriate time.

In later chapters, these building blocks will be discussed in greater detail to offer better clarity on the role they play during decumulation.

1. **Annuities** provide a guaranteed income for life, offering predictability and simplicity. However, they are generally inflexible, and current annuity rates may not always provide the best value for future needs.

2. **Drawdown** plans allow you to keep your pension invested while withdrawing income as needed. This offers flexibility and growth potential but also introduces market risk. Poor sequence-of-returns (bad markets early in retirement) can significantly reduce drawdown income sustainability.

3. **Hybrid** (annuity & drawdown combination) strategies combine the security of an annuity with the adaptability of drawdown, offering a balanced approach.

Naturally, effective planning begins with realistic budgeting and modelling including scenario testing as we have already done above. Tools like Monte Carlo simulations or cashflow modelling software can help test how our plans will perform under different economic and geo-political scenarios.

It goes without saying that tax strategy is critical. In the UK, only 25% of your pension pot is tax-free. Withdrawals beyond this during decumulation may push you into higher tax brackets.

Spreading withdrawals and coordinating with other tax efficient savings like ISAs, Index stocks can improve efficiency.

Finally, review your plan regularly. Life evolves, markets shift, and spending needs change.

Decumulation isn't a "set and forget" process—it's an ongoing activity that requires attention, flexibility, and often, professional guidance as I've already stated.

The following is a practical, structured, Decumulation Personal Planning Checklist to help an individual transform a pension pot into sustainable retirement income spanning several decades:

**1. Define Your Retirement Vision**

- [ ] Determine preferred retirement age
- [ ] Clarify lifestyle expectations (travel, hobbies, caregiving)
- [ ] Consider partial retirement or phased withdrawal from work

**2. Map Your Income Needs**

- [ ] Estimate essential expenses (housing, food, healthcare)
- [ ] Project discretionary costs (entertainment, holidays, family support)
- [ ] Adjust for inflation over time, model and scenario test

**3. Catalogue Income Sources**

- [ ] State Pension (check your forecast here 🔗 https://www.gov.uk/check-national-insurance-record

- [ ] Defined Benefit/Final Salary Schemes
- [ ] Defined Contribution pensions (e.g. drawdown pots)
- [ ] ISAs and other taxable savings
- [ ] Rental, dividend, or part-time income streams

**4. Decide on Withdrawal Approach**

- [ ] Explore annuities for secure income
- [ ] Plan sustainable drawdown (e.g. using e.g. the 4% rule for withdrawals)
- [ ] Build in flexibility for healthcare, emergencies, or large purchases.

**5. Manage and Minimise Risk**

- [ ] Assess the risks and market volatility related to political developments
- [ ] Diversify investments according to your time horizon and risk tolerance
- [ ] Prepare for respite and potential long-term care costs

**6. Optimise Tax Efficiency**

- [ ] Make use of the 25% tax-free pension lump sum
- [ ] Use ISAs and personal allowances wisely
- [ ] Avoid higher tax brackets through careful withdrawal

**7. Plan for the Unexpected**

- [ ] Maintain a minimum of 6 months cash buffer before retiring
- [ ] Review or establish Power of Attorney (health, financial)
- [ ] Watch out for online and offline scams, fraud and financial abuse.

**8. Schedule Regular Reviews**

- [ ] Review withdrawal levels annually
- [ ] Adjust for lifestyle, markets, or legislative changes
- [ ] If deemed necessary, seek professional advice periodically

**9. Consider The Emotional Risks Of Decumulation**

- [ ] Envision Your Retirement Days ('Future History')
- [ ] Identify Your Emotional Anchors (Passions outside of work)?
- [ ] What will be your purpose when you stop being a CIO, teacher etc?
- [ ] Define Your Non-Financial Legacy
- [ ] Practice Decumulation - Try small withdrawals from savings other than your pension pot and *spend them*. How does it make you feel?

A large pension pot enhances retirement potential; however, sustained income depends on how wisely it's managed. Moreover, good planning, a flexible strategy, and regular reviews are what turns a big pot into a good life.

Last but not least, the emotional aspects of retirement are important because retirement is a significant life transition that can trigger emotions good or bad. Certainly, retirement marks a major shift from a structured work life to a more open-ended phase, which can be both exciting and daunting. It's a transition that can impact a person's sense of identity, purpose, and social connections.

# Chapter

# 6 Pension Success Blueprint

It Wasn't Raining When Noah Built The Ark. Be Like Noah

## The Reality Of Planning To Buy A Pension

In my experience, securing a healthy financial future in retirement hinges on early and detailed planning, specifically pension transition planning. Planning is not an event; it is a layering applied at each critical stage of the pension buying process for annuities or income drawdown.

By definition, pension transition planning consists of the scheduled tasks and activities that are to be carried out, when an individual switches from pension saving to pension buying. Compared to pension buying, pension saving is easy, because the real hard work begins with getting access to the pot saved over decades, to secure an individual's financial future in retirement.

Buying a pension is far from being a straightforward task. This is because it involves pulling several levers all at the same time such as choice of provider(s), timing, tax implications, the quality of pension products bought—which must last a person's whole lifetime.

Yet, many people sleepwalk into retirement, either through ignorance or lack of interest or the capacity to tackle the crucial tasks associated with pension transition planning. These tasks often go unaddressed until they're either too late or must be attended to under duress, potentially leading to emotional stress and financial strain.

One common example of this omission is failing to plan ahead to ensure qualification for the full New State Pension (NSP). As many retirees have discovered to their cost, the new full State Pension is not guaranteed—even for those who meet the basic 35 qualifying years criteria.

For instance, if an individual was contracted out under the State Earnings Related Pension Scheme (SERPS) before 2016, they would automatically qualify for the basic State Pension but not the new Additional State Pension, despite meeting the 35-year requirement. This occurs because, during the contracting-out period, some qualifying years were contributed at a lower rate.

I discussed this anomaly in full in a later Chapter under "*State Earnings-Related Pension and The 35 Qualifying Years Trap.*"

**The Cost of Failing to Plan**

An individual who fails to plan properly ahead of retirement risks losing tens of thousands of pounds over their lifetime.

From personal experience, anyone approaching retirement without a transition plan must, in turn, be prepared to endure potential delay to the start of their retirement and possibly loss of income.

This is because the pension purchasing process will almost certainly take longer than anticipated, planned or advised by the provider.

Unless a retiree has contingent savings—as I did—to cushion several months of delays, they will likely experience financial difficulty until receipt of their first pension income. For these and other similar reasons, it's undeniable that transition planning is a key success factor for timely completion of the pension purchase process which triggers the start of pension income.

## The Unpredictable Nature of Retirement Timing

To illustrate how crucial pre-planning was for my retirement transition, I must recount the circumstances that caused me to move my retirement date forward from 2025 to 2023.

In March 2020, just three months into my planning process, the COVID pandemic struck, followed by a worldwide lockdown.

When I began planning, a five-year glide path from 2020-2025 seemed like ample time—allowing me to proceed steadily and methodically, ensuring every detail was thoroughly covered.

Then, COVID turned the world upside down, unleashing social and economic volatility, uncertainty, complexity, and ambiguity—the likes of which had never taken place before in peacetime.

Against the background of the uncertainties created by COVID, I resolved to use the SMART Framework—a simple but effective planning tool—to ensure my planning was methodical, thorough and structured layer by layer.

My first task was to request the latest statement for each of my seven pension pots. I wanted to know how much my pension pots were worth, how their value has changed over time and, using the current balance, estimate the income that I could expect in retirement using any of the pension calculators available online.

My statements (not projections) indicated my pots continued to perform very well and if I carried on working until 2025, I would at some point in 2023 surpass the LTA limit of £1.073,100 (£1.07 million). It was about this time that I decided I would retire on 31 March 2023 rather than wait until 2025.

At the time, exceeding the LTA would trigger tax penalties of 55% if the excess was taken as a lump sum, or 25% plus my marginal rate of income tax of 45%, if I'd taken it as any other form of pension benefits, such as through drawdown or when buying an annuity.

Both scenarios were complications that I didn't need. However, there was a sting in the tail of the LTA regulation which further reinforces why some personal familiarity with headline pension rules and financial advice are always desirable.

Completely out of the blue on March 15, 2023, barely 16 days before the start of my retirement, the then Chancellor of the Exchequer Jeremy Hunt MP, announced the abolition of the LTA from 6 April 2024!

Without a shadow of a doubt, without the structured plans I had developed from January 2020 onwards, my transition to retirement would have been extremely challenging—both financially and in terms of effort.

## SMART Framework For Planning

The SMART framework is a widely used management method for setting effective goals in various fields, from pension financial planning and personal development to project management.

This framework provides clarity and motivation, ensuring efficiency when carrying out tasks and activities. Crucially, it ensures that objectives are clear, actionable, and realistic by following five key criteria:

**Specific** – Goals should be precise and well-defined to eliminate ambiguity. For example, instead of saying, "put away some money every month," a SMART goal would be, *"Save £200 on the last working day of every month until 2030."*

**Measurable** – Progress should be trackable through tangible metrics or milestones. For instance, *"By 2030 my savings including interest must be at least £13,000"* provides a clear target or objective.

**Achievable** – Goals must be challenging but realistic, taking into consideration available resources. An individual grossing monthly earnings of £1,500 per month wouldn't set a monthly savings target like: "Save £750.00 monthly," but *"Save £200.00 monthly" is more feasible.*

**Relevant** – Objectives should align with broader aspirations or specific personal goals. If a person wishes to retire at the age of 55, a relevant SMART goal would be: *"By my 55th birthday, my pension pot must be worth a minimum £750,000."*

**Time-bound** – Setting deadlines creates urgency and accountability. Instead of saying, "I will retire in my 50s," a SMART goal would be, *"I will retire on my 55th birthday."*

Finally, it's worth remembering that planning and doing grows in the soil of action, not in the barren and bad lands of good intentions.

### Benefits of Using the SMART Framework

SMART framework enhances focus, facilitates ownership, simplifies and clarifies objectives—ultimately increasing the chances of successfully accomplishing any set targets or goals.

**Figure 8.0 The SMART Framework**

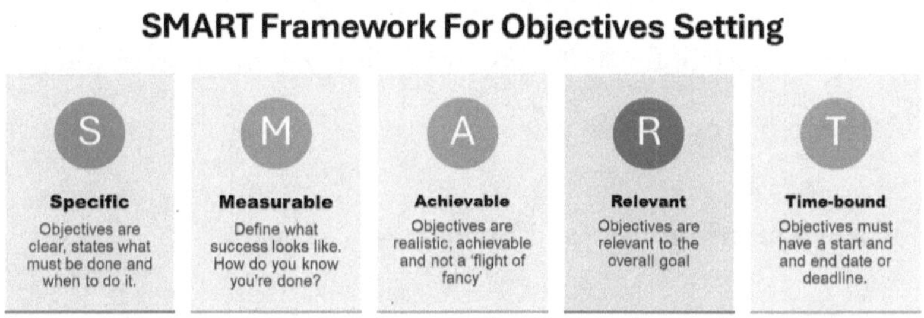


SMART goals and objectives are ultimately broken down into simple tasks and activities, forming a critical path of actionable steps to get a desired result.

### Using SMART Framework To Buy Annuity or Enter Drawdown

Applying the SMART framework to pension decisions (annuities vs. drawdown) transforms vague retirement plans into actionable strategies.

**Here's how:-**

**1. Specific: Define Exactly What You Want**

📌**Annuity Goal:**

Guaranteed £15,000/year essential income (indexed to inflation) plus State Pension starting at age 67, lasting for life.

📌**Drawdown Goal:**

Withdraw *4% annually (£20,000/year) from a £500,000 pension pot, adjusted for inflation, while leaving the rest of the pot invested. **(i.e. The 4% rule).*

📌**Key Questions To Ask Yourself:**

- What's your essential vs. discretionary spending?

- Do you prioritize stability (annuity) over flexibility (drawdown)?

**2. Measurable: Quantify Targets & Progress**

📌**Annuity Metrics:**

- Compare quotes for £15,000/year income (e.g. £200,000 purchase price).

- Track inflation linkage if required (e.g. RPI+2%).

📌**Drawdown Metrics:**

- Use the "4% rule" (i.e. withdraw 4% of your pot in the 1st year of retirement).

- Monitor portfolio value quarterly (e.g. never dip below £400,000).

📌 Helpful Tools:

**- Annuities: Standard Life**

🔗https://www.standardlife.co.uk/retirement/tools/retirement-calculator

**- Drawdown: Fowler Drew**

Drew🔗https://fowlerdrew.co.uk/drawdown-planner/

**3. Achievable: Align with Realistic Resources**

📌**Annuity Feasibility:**

- Can my pension pot buy the desired income? (e.g. £200,000 needed for £15,000/year annuity at 67).

- Health conditions? Enhanced annuities pay 10-40% more for illnesses.

📌**Drawdown Feasibility:**

- Is my pot large enough to sustain withdrawals? (e.g. £500,000 for £20,000/year at 4%).

- **Test scenarios:** 2022-style 20% market drop cuts income to £16,000.

Also, post Trump Trade Tariff announcement of April 2025, when the market fell 12% as S&P 500 companies lost U.S. $5.8 trillion!

📌**Red Flags:**

- Drawdown may require a minimum pot size (e.g. £100K+ for feasibility).

- Annuity is of poor value in the event of short life expectancy.

**4. Relevant: Match to Personal Priorities**

📌**Behavioural Fit:**

- **Risk-averse?** Annuity reduces anxiety.

- **Market-savvy?** Drawdown offers control.

**Figure 9.0 Personal Priorities: Annuity v Drawdown**

| Priorities | Annuity Better For | Drawdown Better For |
|---|---|---|
| **Income Certainty** | ✅Guaranteed *lifelong income unless *term annuity bought | ❌Market risk |
| **Flexibility** | ❌Irreversible | ✅Adjust withdrawals yearly |
| **Legacy** | ❌Usually no *inheritance unless joint life annuity bought | ✅Unspent funds are passed to estate or heirs |
| **Inflation Protection** | ✅With index-linking add-on | ❌Requires manual intervention |

### 5. Time-bound: Set Deadlines & Review Points

📌**Annuity Timeline:**

- Deadline: Purchase by age 75 (UK tax efficiency).

- Review: Revisit quotes 6 months pre-retirement as part of transition plan.

📌**Drawdown Timeline:**

- Annual Review: Adjust withdrawals based on portfolio performance.

- Trigger Points: Reduce income if pot falls below £450,000.

📌**Critical Dates:**

- State Pension age (e.g. 66 UK, 67 Australia, 65 Canada, 65 New Zealand, 66 United States but full retirement age (FRA) varies depending on year of birth).

**6.0 SMART Hybrid Strategy Example**

**Combined annuity/drawdown for a balanced, hybrid portfolio.**

📌E.g. Use £150,000 to buy an inflation-linked annuity covering essentials (£10,000/year). Withdraw 3.5% annually (£12,250/year) from remaining £350,000 drawdown pot for discretionary spending. Review drawdown rate every 3 years.

**7.0 Pitfalls to Avoid**

📌**Annuities:**

- Not shopping around (losing 20%+ income).

- Ignoring inflation (e.g. £15,000 fixed today = £8,300 in 30 years at 3% inflation).

📌**Drawdown:**

- Overestimating sustainable withdrawal rates.

- Underestimating longevity (30% of 65-year-olds live to 90+).

**8.0 Potential Action Plan (Informational Only)**

🚨 Self Audit: Calculate essential annual income (e.g. housing, food).

🚨 Model: Use pension calculators to test annuity vs. drawdown outcomes.

🚨 Insure: Cover longevity risk with partial annuity.

🚨 Review: Formal annual check with a financial advisor, especially for individuals with drawdown income.

By making your pension goals SMART, you turn uncertainty into a planned roadmap – ensuring your retirement income is stress-tested, adaptable, and aligned with your personal lifestyle.

**Common Mistakes When Setting SMART Objectives**

When setting SMART goals, it's easy to make certain mistakes that can hinder progress and make goals and objectives less SMART. Listed below are some common mistakes to look out for:

📌**Being too vague** – Even within the SMART framework, some goals may remain unclear. Ensure objectives are specific enough to eliminate ambiguity.

📌**Ignoring measurability** – If you can't track progress, it's hard to stay motivated or on course. Use hard metrics or milestones to measure success.

📌**Setting unrealistic goals** – Overly ambitious targets can be discouraging and can frustrate the best laid plans. Know your resources and mind your constraints.

📌**Failing to set a timeline** – Without deadlines, motivation may dwindle. On a more practical level, failing to set a timeline for completion of buying annuity or enter drawdown is asking for financial trouble.

📌**Not aligning with broader objectives** – Goals that don't support personal priorities and objectives may become distractions rather than improvements.

📌**Not reviewing and adjusting** – Circumstances change. Failing to reassess goals can lead to wasted effort, irrelevant pursuits or financial loss.

📌**Skipping a plan of action** – SMART goals are great, but without a step-by-step plan, delivering the goals or objectives becomes difficult.

Avoiding these mistakes can keep goals and objectives effective and focused.

**SMART Workflow: CREDO, Workplans & Work Instruction**

During my pension buying application process, I created three-tiered template forms and documents (they're included in later chapters in the book), which I used to organize my SMART CREDO, goals, objectives and tasks into a simple workflow. Each document brought a different level of organisation and discipline to the identification of goals, objects and finally tasks to be executed.

The three Form templates and their use cases & applications are as follows:-

✅ CREDO - Used to define overarching retirement Aspirations

✅ Workplan - This template form listed my SMART Goals and Objectives

✅ Work Instruction - This workhorse form captured SMART Tasks/To-Do-List

**Figure 10.0 CREDO, Workplan & Work Instruction**

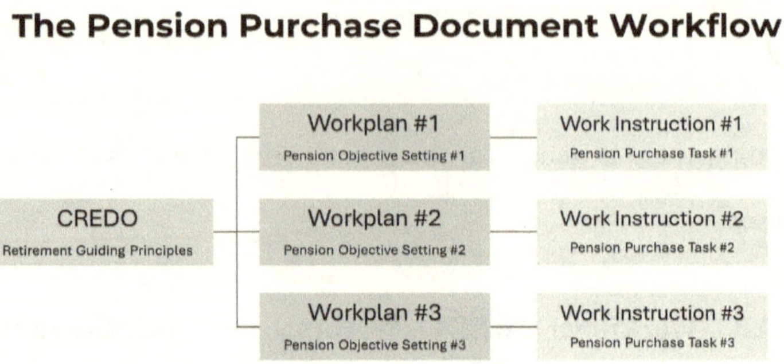


The documents in the workflow for pension buying/drawdown are described below.

**CREDO - Top Level Workflow Document**

The CREDO was the first planning document created when I kicked off my pension purchase activities. It stated my overarching mission and nothing else. The CREDO was the 30,000 feet view of my retirement aspirations.

✅ The CREDO was designed as a one-off, mission/errand definition document.

✅ It serves as an overarching, succinct, and unambiguous aspirational guide.

✅ Once established, every subsequent task flows from it.

Below is the actual CREDO that I used to plan my pension purchase/drawdown.

**Figure 11.0 CREDO - Example: Credo Document**

> ☐ 'I will retire on 31 March 2023. By this date, all my direct and indirect pension affairs will be in order, and I will be debt free. I will start drawing monthly retirement income from April 2023 onwards.'

CREDO was clear and self-explanatory, but in essence, it identified four main goals—each representing a non-negotiable priority unless disrupted by an "Act of God" like COVID-19 or a similar unforeseen event:

📌**The four goals were as follows:-**

✅ (a) My immovable retirement date. *(i.e. 31 March 2023)*

✅(b) The organization of my pension affairs, including NI qualification status and any necessary follow-ups. *(i.e. put pension affairs in order).*

✅ (c) The projected state of my financial affairs at a future date. *(i.e. debt free)*

✅ (d) The immovable date when my pension income would commence, aligned with the cessation of my professional working life. *(i.e. April 2023)*

Here's the essential point. My CREDO served as the mission statement—defining retirement as the goal, establishing guiding principles, and marking the critical dates for initiating and completing the process.

**Workplan - Second Level Workflow Document**

The Workplan is the 5,000 feet view of my high-level, CREDO goals; but it does not contain task level details held in the Work Instruction.

**Figure 12.00 Workplan 1- Demo Second Level Goals/Objectives**

| Criteria | Description |
|---|---|
| **(S)** | Define the goal clearly and precisely. |
| **Specific** | **Example:** To be completely debt free as follows: Credit cards, mortgage, bank loan; vehicle hire purchase; other outstanding financing." |
| **(M)** | Ensure the goal can be measured. In other words, it's what success looks like. |
| **Measurable** | **Example:** "All outstanding debts must be paid down to zero or nil balance." |
| **(A)** | Ensure the goal is realistic and achievable. |
| **Achievable** | **Example:** "Allocate funds from the family budget to clear outstanding credit card debt." |
| **(R)** | Make sure the goal aligns with broader pension goals. |
| **Relevant** | **Example:** "Debt reduction to zero balance aligns with debt free aspiration on reaching retirement." |
| **(T)** | **Set a clear deadline for goal completion.** |
| **Time-bound** | **Example:** "Starting March 2020, pay off all outstanding debt by March 31st, 2023." |

**Work Instruction - Third Level Workflow Document**

My Work Instruction was the 10 feet view. It was a detailed, To-Do-List itemizing individual tasks that must be carried out in order to successfully reach a goal or deliver an objective.

**Figure 13.0 Work Instruction - 3rd Level To-Do-List Example**

| **Work Instruction 001 - National Insurance (NI) Top-Up** | |
|---|---|
| **Work Instruction No** | 001 |
| **Start and End Dates** | January 4th - January 10th |
| **Work Instruction Type** | National Insurance (NI) Top-Up - To determine qualification status for full State Pension. If your National Insurance record started before April 2016, you will need 35 qualifying years to get the full rate of the new State Pension. |

| **Work Instruction (To Do List)** | Apply to HMRC for Govt. Gateway user ID if you don't already have one. Otherwise use your login via the URL below. 🔗 https://www.access.service.gov.uk/login/signin/creds<br><br>The link takes you to the 'National Insurance' page, from there click the 'Check your national insurance contribution' link which takes you to 'Your NI Records' page.<br><br>'Your NI Records' shows how many full years contributions were made and how many 'Year Not In Full' contributions there are.<br><br>Based on your personal circumstances and current legislation, you may wish to 'top up' any gaps to increase your State Pension entitlement.<br><br>You should take professional advice if you're unsure whether or not topping up is worth your while. Start with Pension Wise free on 📞0800 011 3797 or free 🔗 use our webchat<br><br>https://www.moneyhelper.org.uk/PensionsChat |
|---|---|

While a CREDO theoretically defined the aspirational destination, it was the SMART Goals/Objective Workplan and SMART Work Instruction, that:

✅ Identified individual essential tasks or To-Do-List.

✅ Sequenced activities logically.

✅ Ensured completion of critical tasks before moving on to the next one or pension buying/drawdown stage.

**Retirement Brought Forward to 31 March 2023**

In January 2023, I accelerated my retirement timeline by two years to 2023, officially retiring on 31 March of that year. I've already gone into great detail why I did so, but primarily it had to do with the size of my combined pots relative to the Lifetime Allowance which I was in danger of surpassing.

Looking back, bringing forward my retirement by two years to 2023 would have been difficult to execute, without the retirement transition plan that I had methodically developed since January 2020, and the templates discussed above.

Given this unexpected change, I cannot in all good conscience overemphasize how crucial the combination of my CREDO, SMART Goals, SMART Objectives (Workplans), and Work Instruction workflow-documentation were.

Similarly to the above examples, when buying a pension in retirement or when planning to enter drawdown, meeting timeliness and success rested on the plan I built using the three planning documents described in this chapter.

In Chapter 8 Pensions Information Discovery, the forms were used extensively to capture real life information and data required for pension buying or for drawdown income.

Depending on how many pension pots an individual has, they may be asked to provide the information captured in the Work Instructions in Chapter 6 numerous times to different providers; and having the information in one Work Instruction will save a ton of time!

By storing the information required by providers in Work Instructions, it was an easy task to retrieve and present the information to a 3rd party in a consistent and accurate manner every time.

Bearing in mind the information provided by a pension saver is used by the providers Actuary to calculate pension income, it is contractually and legally binding that any information provided must be accurate and true.

Chapter

# 7 Avoiding Pension Scams And Frauds

Miracles Like Deals With The Devil Come With Strings Attached

## The Growing Threat Of Pension Frauds And Scams

Pension fraud has multiplied in recent years, evolving into a significant industry and posing a serious threat to consumers and institutions—private and public.

With scammers employing increasingly sophisticated tactics, they target unsuspecting and vulnerable organisations and individuals, seeking to exploit the growing complexity of pension schemes. As pension pots multiply, fraudsters continuously find new ways to manipulate the system, deceiving individuals into parting with their hard-earned savings.

### A True-to-Life Scenario: How Pension Scammers Operate

🚨 Picture this situation or scenario: You've worked diligently for over 35 years, carefully building a substantial pension pot.

Now, just three years away from retirement, you unexpectedly receive an unsolicited call from a supposed 'pension expert'. The caller confidently promises to unlock your pension early and "transfer" it into a much sought after 'high-performance fund'. The scammer's pitch and claim were rather convincing and went something like this:-

✅ Your pension savings will be placed in a "flexible," "innovative," and "high growth" investment fund.

✅ The fund boasts a track record of double-digit growth, year after year, with the potential to double the value of your pension pot in two to three years.

✅ To further gain the person's trust the caller openly admits they will receive an introduction fee—a subtle yet effective ploy to create a false sense of security.

However, the harsh reality is that such fraudsters simply take your money and disappear, leaving you penniless, with no recourse to recover your funds.

### A Personal Experience: Facing Pension Scams Firsthand

Are you still with me? It's important that you are. The scenario above was not hypothetical—it was one of several scams I personally fended off in recent years.

**Figure 14.0 Pension Wise - Anti-Scam Warning**

### Scams: If It Sounds Too Good to Be True It Probably Is

Clearly, if any of the claims made above sounded too good to be true, that's because they probably were.

Virtually all "get-rich-quick" schemes, especially those proposed by unsolicited or cold callers promising to double a person's pension pot over a short period of time, are in all likelihood, scams and fraudulent.

Fraudsters prey on individuals who may be financially vulnerable, and unfortunately, millions of people globally—many approaching retirement—fall into this category.

### My Personal Experience with Pension Scammers

The scenario I described above was neither hypothetical nor theoretical. It happened to me!

In April 2020, I received my first attempt from unknown individuals trying to steal my pension, just as I was on the 'last mile' to retirement. But it wasn't the only time fraudsters attempted—and failed—to gain access to my pension pots.

At least two or three similar attempts were made over a 12-month period. Below are several accounts of scammers and fraudsters attempting to scam me out of my pension pots.

## July 2020: The 2nd Scam Attempt—Pension Unlocking Fraud

In July 2020, another attempt was made to steal my pensions—again via a cold caller.

This time, the scam involved a "pension unlocking fraud", where the scammer promised early access to my pension savings before the legal retirement age of 55 (rising to 57 from April 2028).

To make the offer more enticing, the caller dangled a tempting 'golden hello' cash bonus, allegedly to help tackle any immediate or current financial concerns. The fraudster began by asking me to confirm a series of personal details, including the following:

❌ Full name

❌ Date of birth (DOB)

❌ Full address

❌ National Insurance (NI) number

I refused outright to confirm or deny any personal information to the caller.

Since the scammer had called me—rather than the other way around—I made it clear that I would not provide any personal details before the cold caller abruptly rang off. There's a good reason why I never confirm or deny personal details to cold callers—something that I will cover later.

Even setting aside the risk of losing my pension pots, and potentially severe financial consequences, including hefty tax penalties, had the fraudster done their homework, they would have realised I was older than 55 at the time!

**December 2020: The 3rd Scam Attempt—Fake SIPPs Scheme**

The third and final scam attempt I recall receiving was in December 2020, just a couple of weeks before Christmas, as I recovered from COVID19.

Yet again, it was an unsolicited call—this time from a woman claiming that my name had been passed to her as part of an exclusive list of people coming up for retirement.

She claimed that her company's Self-Invested Personal Pension (SIPP) was growing at an incredible rate, and all I had to do was transfer my pension pot into the scheme via her brokerage firm.

Coincidentally, I already had a SIPP with the very provider she claimed to represent or work for. I had a moment of epiphany at that point that it was a scam! Without saying another word, I hung up purposely and deliberately.

Burdened by COVID, I was more miffed that the scammer had sapped what little energy I had left as I recovered, than with her fraudulent call which was never going anywhere in view of my background and experience with online and offline fraudsters.

**Data Privacy & Security in the 21st Century: Why It Matters**

After experiencing three attempted scams in just eight months, I began to wonder how fraudsters and scammers had obtained my personal and contact details.

That was when I recalled the major data breaches that had occurred in recent years, including:

✅ Microsoft (2020)—where I was also a client

✅ Capital One (2019)—where I was a customer

✅ Yahoo (2013)—Considered the largest data breach in history, over 3 billion Yahoo user accounts were hacked! Even worse, the hack went undetected for three years!

Coincidentally, I had a Yahoo account at the time of the breach. Interestingly, one of the most notorious cyberattacks of the last two decades occurred in July 2015, when Ashley Madison, the online extra-marital affairs website was hacked! The Ashley Madison breach which I've discussed below was fascinating for the wrong reasons, but chiefly because it brought home to consumers one of the unforeseen consequences and dangers of data breach: potential threats to themselves, their family and marriage relationship.

**Ashley Madison Data Breach**

Ashley Madison is an online dating and social networking service marketed toward people in relationships or marriages seeking extramarital affairs.

*"Life is short. Have an affair,"* goes the bold slogan by Ashley Madison, a Canadian dating website aimed exclusively at married couples. And millions around the world took the company up on their offer.

In 2015, Ashley Madison predictably suffered a massive data breach, publicly exposing the personal details of its users. The hackers published the email addresses of 37 million Ashley Madison members online.

While the exact number of users per country was not known, Canada, Britain and the U.S. saw the most significant repercussions (i.e. marital breakups) due to the large user base and the subsequent public exposure of user information. Other countries affected were:-

- ✅ Australia
- ✅ Brazil
- ✅ Canada

Due to the scale and salacious nature of the exposure, the Ashley Madison hack quickly dominated global headlines, making it one of the most talked about data breaches over the last 20 years!

Following the attack, data security and personal privacy violations became hotly debated topics among ordinary consumers. It was the only silver lining out of a messy, disruptive hack.

Although the hack resulted in massive personal consequences, it also had a positive impact and heightening public awareness of:

- ✅ The dangers of online security failures
- ✅ The risks of identity theft
- ✅ The long-term consequences of compromised data

**The Motives Behind the Ashley Madison Hack**

As the Ashley Madison crisis unfolded, it became apparent that those responsible for the hack were not financially motivated.

**There was no evidence of:**

❌ Financial extortion

❌ Fraud

❌ Data brokerage

Even though the hackers had access to millions of customer financial records, no fraudulent scams took place, but they had other plans.

✅ To pressure Ashley Madison into changing its business model.

✅ To publicly embarrass its users.

Was My Data Compromised? No silly😆, was yours? Seriously, I wasn't referring to Ashley Madison, although like many consumers, I was a customer of several other major online platforms, including the following:

✅ Capital One

✅ Microsoft

✅ Amazon

✅ Yahoo

✅ Apple

✅ Twitter (now 'X')

✅ WhatsApp

Given the frequency of large-scale cyberattacks, it would not be unreasonable to assume that my personal data had at one time, or another been harvested from one of the many online services I used.

To be clear, I am not alleging that any of the companies listed above were involved in leaking my personal data. However, given the nature of digital information, it was inevitable that unauthorized individuals would gain access to my personal data at some point.

**My Background in Information Technology and Data Security**

Professionally, I had a strong background in securing information technology systems and data on high transaction, database management platforms. As a former CIO and Technology Director at Manchester Airports Group, I was responsible for safeguarding mission critical airport infrastructure for border and passenger security, sensitive data, including information on VIPs viz:

- ✅ Former Prime Minister Tony Blair and his Cabinet
- ✅ The late Former Deputy Prime Minister John Prescott
- ✅ Richard Branson
- ✅ The late Queen Elizabeth II
- ✅ The Red Arrows

Additionally, I led the implementation or delivery of GDPR-compliant security systems and managed major enterprise technology deployments at:

✅ Vodafone Global Enterprise (VGE)

✅ Landis+Gyr

Given my extensive experience in cybersecurity, I understood—more than most—the dangers posed by compromised personal data when unauthorized individuals gain access with the intent to commit fraud or steal sensitive information.

Consequently, as a rule of the thumb, I never shared personal details over the phone—especially with cold callers—unless I had initiated the call personally.

This guiding principle stemmed from the firm conviction that divulging personal details to unknown individuals would eventually lead to compromised data.

**Guidelines for Protecting Personal Information Offline**

**1. Avoid Using Your Given Name Unless Contractually Needful**

My first line of defence against identity theft is never to confirm or deny my given name or personal details when asked by a cold caller.

The only exceptions are interactions with double-verified entities, such as:

✅ My bank

✅ My pension provider

✅ HMRC

✅ DVLA

For anyone unfamiliar with the terminology, a given name (GN) refers to the name on an individual's birth certificate. Instead of providing my given name in frivolous or non-contractual situations, I always use my common name (CN) or alias.

📌 Examples of **Common Names (CN)** *versus* **Given Names (GN)**

- **"Kiki Anderson"** = instead of "Michaela Anderson"
- **"Bola Ishola"** = instead of "Adebola Ishola"
- **"Bob Jones"** = instead of "Robert Alwyn Jones"
- **"Pum Mandinka"** = instead of "Pumba Nikolozi Mandinka"

**Why Use Common Name for Frivolous Transactions?**

In order to gain access to one of my pension pots during my pension purchasing process, I inadvertently used my common name instead of my full given name during my provider's offline security verification process.

✅ The provider flagged a mismatch between my CN and GN, thus prevented the buying process from progressing beyond that point.

✅ When I realized my error, I corrected it by providing my given name, which allowed me to clear security verification at the second attempt.

📌**Since then, this has remained my default practice:**

✔ Given name = Contractually binding agreements

✔ Common name = Non-contractual transactions, both online and offline

**2. Never Divulge Your Date of Birth to Unknown Callers**

Avoid sharing your date of birth (DOB) over the phone or online unless:

✅ You initiated the call

✅ The entity is a trusted, double-verified organization

🚨 **Why This Matters**

❌ A date of birth combined with a name creates a significant personal data vulnerability, often exploited by fraudsters and scammers.

❌ **Identity theft can have severe consequences, including:**

- Financial compromise
- Reputational damage
- Loss of benefits
- Legal issues

**Victims of Identity theft may also experience:**

⚠️ Adverse credit scores

⚠️ Emotional distress

⚠️ Difficulty accessing essential services, like mortgage approvals

⚠️ Bank account fraud, where scammers withdraw or empty funds

**3. Never Share Home Address or Postcode with Cold Callers**

Unless I initiated or prearranged the call, I never confirm or deny my home address or postcode to cold callers.

📌 **Why?**

✅ The correct combination of address and postcode can be exploited for identity impersonation, just like a DOB and given name.

**4. You May Trust Known Callers But Always Verify**

If I received a call from someone claiming to represent my bank, insurance company, or pension provider, I always:

✔ Request their name and a reference number for the call.

✔ Wait at least 10 minutes before calling back (*to avoid call forwarding fraud*).

✔ Use a stored phone number from my contacts to call back the organization.

🚨 **Call Interception & Rerouting Fraud**

Fraudsters can use interception techniques to redirect outgoing or incoming calls to fake reroute numbers, gaining unauthorized access to personal details

**Managing the Threat of Identity Theft**

I cannot overstate the importance of protecting personal data. You should bear in mind that as a potential victim of fraud or a scam, you have to be successful at preventing fraud or scams 100% of the time. By contrast, a fraudster or scammer only has to be lucky 1% of the time. In fraud, the difference between 100% and 1% is razor thin because that 1% could cost you your entire life savings!

**Beyond financial loss, identity theft can cause:**

❌ Severe damage to credit reputation

❌ Lengthy recovery processes

**According to the U.S. Federal Trade Commission (FTC):**

🚨 Recovering from identity theft can take approximately six months

🚨 Resolution might require up to 200 hours of solid, professional aided work

**The Growing Risks of Pension Scams and Fraud Globally**

Unfortunately, identity theft and fraudulent pension transfers are widespread, affecting hundreds of thousands of people in Britain annually as well as in the rest of the world.

According to studies from the UK's Citizens Advice Bureau and ONS data:

⚠️ In the UK, the cost-of-living crisis has exacerbated financial fraud, making scams more prevalent.

⚠️ Many individuals approaching retirement have been conned out of their life savings through a variety of fraudulent schemes.

**The Shift to Digital Pension Statements and Management**

Three years before retirement, I found out that all my pension pots were accessible online—a testament to digital transformation efforts by UK pension providers. Indeed, some providers charged higher fees to non-digital savers.

Unfortunately, digitisation of pensions or moving pensions online was a double edge sword. While it simplified rapid access to pension statements and other user activities, at the same time it made it easy for scammers to gain easy access to pension pots with lax security.

This is one of the reasons why every person, especially pensioners with large savings, should prioritize data privacy as a non-negotiable habit.

**Personally, I welcomed the flexibility of online pension access:**

✅ Gone was the requirement to talk to AI 24/7 on automated switchboards.

✅ No need to sort through pages of material documents.

✅ Convenient investment tracking anytime, anyplace and anywhere.

✅ Ability to transfer pension funds digitally in minutes.

For someone like me, with a strong information technology background, accessing my pension pots online was a game-changer!

**Challenges for Baby Boomers in Digital Pension Management**

Despite my ease with technology, I would suspect my affinity with digitisation is atypical among members of my generation and even older ones—particularly Baby Boomers (those *born between 1946 and 1964*).

Unfortunately, many pension savers lack digital literacy in the following areas:-

❌ Knowledge of online security best practices especially around personal data

❌ Understanding of cybersecurity risks

❌ Awareness of data protection protocols

This knowledge gap makes many Baby Boomers and seniors vulnerable to:

⚠️ Phishing emails, designed to steal sensitive information

⚠️ Fake pension websites, tricking users into submitting login credentials

⚠️ Hacks into pension providers' systems, leading to large-scale data breach

⚠️ Fraudulent pension transfer schemes, where scammers impersonate legitimate providers

⚠️ Vishing—short for voice phishing—is a type of scam where fraudsters use phone calls or voice messages to trick people into revealing personal data

Regrettably, as digital pension platforms continue to grow, online fraud will inevitably increase.

**Common Online Pension Scams**

Many people fall victim to phishing attacks, either:

❌ Through email scams.

❌ By unknowingly handing over login credentials online or over the phone.

**This might allow scammers to:**

⚠️ Steal pension savings and other financial assets

⚠️ Commit identity fraud

⚠️ Impersonate the victim in order to defraud their friends and/or family

## HMRC Phishing Attacks In 2016 and 2025

In 2016, the HMRC self-assessment database for UK taxpayers was breached by cybercriminals in a phishing attack.

Unfortunately, some of the scammers went on to successfully submit fraudulent tax repayment claims using stolen taxpayer identities. I first became aware of this hack when my Hampshire-based accountant called to inform me that HMRC had notified him that my self-assessment records had been hacked!

Apart from my own information, tens of thousands of other taxpayer records were hacked using stolen identity and authentication data.

While HMRC did not disclose the exact number of successful fraudulent claims, it was clear that the losses ran into hundreds of thousands—if not millions—of pounds.

Around the same time, The Sunday Times reported that, in the previous year alone, HMRC had prevented approximately 17,000 fraud attempts, stopping an estimated £100 million in fraudulent claims!

### 🚨 Hot Pick: HMRC Cyber Attacks 2025

HMRC's internal security systems detected unauthorised access to some taxpayers' online accounts. This was an attempt to claim money from HMRC, not an attempt to take any money directly from taxpayers.

HMRC subsequently wrote to affected taxpayers and took action to protect these accounts. How effective HMRC's precautions are, only time will tell!

**The HMRC Hacks Proved the Most Cautious Can Be Affected**

There was a certain irony in discovering that *my* HMRC record was among those breached during the 2016 cyberattack. Of all the accounts they could've hacked to make a fraudulent claim—they chose mine.

Despite doing everything in my power to protect myself from cyber fraud, I still became an unwitting casualty—caught in the blast radius when HMRC's tax returns systems were breached. Through no fault of my own, I was pulled into the very scenario I'd worked so hard to avoid.

**The moral of this incident is crystal clear:**

🚨 Despite your best efforts you may still fall victim to scams via a 3rd party

🚨 Online scammers only need to get lucky once

🚨 Potential victims must be lucky one hundred percent of the time

I know what you're thinking: "Luck? What has luck got to do with cybersecurity?"

Well, you're correct but only up to a point—cybersecurity luck doesn't just fall from the sky, you have to make your own luck.

A powerful way to do just that is by following the guidance laid out by the U.S. Cybersecurity and Infrastructure Security Agency (CISA)—a trusted source for proactive protection in an increasingly digital and fraudulent world.

✅ Use strong passwords: a combination of characters, numbers, letter case.

✅ Regularly update your software.

✅ Think before clicking on suspicious links.

✅ Enable multi-factor authentication (MFA).

These cyber hygiene practices, applicable to both individuals and organizations, may drastically improve online safety and security.

**Common Pension Scams, Red Flags, and Preventive Measures**

Below, I've compiled a matrix table identifying common pension scams, warning signs, and strategies for protection.

The list below covers nearly the full spectrum of online, offline scams and frauds primarily targeted at pension savers coming up to retirement.

Such scams include old hands like 'Early Pension Release (aka "Pension Liberation")', 'Investment Fraud', 'Clone Firms', 'Free Pension Reviews', 'Fake Pension Scams' and 'Employer Related *Scams' and so on and so forth.

The matrix lists over thirty scams including their variants and flavours in one form or another.

🚨 **Disclaimer**

- The examples below are for informational purposes only.
- They neither constitute security nor financial advice.

**Figure 15.0 Summary of Common Scams & Deterrents**

| Types of Frauds & Scams | Red Flags | How To Protect Yourself |
|---|---|---|
| **Identity Theft** | 1/. Suspicious activity on bank accounts or credit cards<br><br>2/. Unexpected bills or deliveries<br><br>3/. Mail addressed to unknown individuals.<br><br>4/. Denial of credit applications | a/. Protect your personal information: Shred sensitive documents, use strong passwords, and be cautious about sharing personal details online.<br><br>b/. Monitor your accounts regularly: Check bank statements, credit card |

| | | |
|---|---|---|
| | 5/. Receiving calls or emails about suspicious activities on your accounts<br><br>6/. Finding personal information online or in public places | bills, and credit reports for any unusual activity<br><br>c/. Be wary of phishing emails and calls (vishing): Do not click on links or open attachments in suspicious emails<br><br>d/. Use strong passwords and enable two-factor authentication<br><br>e/. Report any suspected identity theft to the relevant authorities |
| **Free Pension Review Scam** | 1/. High-pressure sales tactics: Urging immediate | a/. Never engage with unsolicited contact: Hang up on cold calls |

| | | |
|---|---|---|
| | decisions with limited time offers.<br><br>2/. Focus on switching pension provider not pensions advice: Emphasizing transferring your pension rather than providing a holistic review<br><br>3/. Unrealistic or too good to be true promises: Guaranteeing high returns with little or no risk<br><br>4/. Lack of transparency: Difficulty understanding the | and ignore unsolicited emails or texts<br><br>b/. Research thoroughly: Check the FCA register to verify the company and individual's authorization.<br><br>c/. Obtain multiple quotes: Compare offers from different, reputable providers<br><br>d/. Seek independent advice: Consult with a qualified, FCA-regulated pension adviser.<br><br>e/. Be wary of "free" offers: Understand the |

| | | |
|---|---|---|
| | costs involved with a "free" review<br><br>5/. Online advertising: Prominent ads on social media or search engines with vague promises | potential costs and implication |
| **Pension Liberation Scam** | 1/. **Early access promises:** Offering to release your pension before your 55th birthday (57 from April 2028)<br><br>2/. **Focus on tax-free lump sums**: Emphasizing accessing your | a/. Understand pension rules: Familiarize yourself with the rules around accessing your pension.<br>b/. Consult with a qualified adviser: Discuss your options with an FCA-regulated pension specialist.<br><br>c/. Be wary of unrealistic promises: |

| | | |
|---|---|---|
| | pension tax-free, ignoring long-term consequences<br><br>3/. **High fees and charges:** Significant charges for accessing your pension early, are often hidden and unclear<br><br>4/. **Lack of FCA authorization:** The Firm or individual is not authorized to provide pension advice<br><br>5/. **Social media hype:** Prominent promotion of "pension | Early access to your pension often has significant downsides and tax implications<br>d/. Consider long-term implications: Assess the impact of early access on your retirement income<br><br>e/. Never make hasty decisions: Take your time, research thoroughly, and seek professional guidance |

| | | |
|---|---|---|
| | liberation" schemes on social media platforms using deep fake videos of famous people. | |
| **Investment Scams within Pensions** | 1/. **High-risk investments:** Recommending unsuitable high-risk investments within your pension<br><br>2/. **Lack of diversification:** Concentrating your investments in a single asset or sector<br><br>3/.**Misrepresentation of risks:** | a/. Understand your risk tolerance: Assess your ability and willingness to accept investment risk<br>b/. Diversify your portfolio: Spread your investments across different asset classes and sectors<br><br>c/. Review your investments regularly: Monitor your portfolio's performance and make adjustments as needed |

|  |  |  |
|---|---|---|
|  | Downplaying or ignoring the potential risks associated with investments.<br><br>4/. **Conflicting interests:** The adviser may benefit from recommending certain investments.<br><br>5/. **Lack of ongoing monitoring**: Failing to review & adjust your investment strategy over time. | d/. Seek independent advice: Consult with a qualified, fee-based adviser who acts in your best interests<br><br>e/. Be wary of overly complex or aggressive investment strategies. |

| | | |
|---|---|---|
| **Online Frauds and Phishing Attacks** | 1/. Emails or texts or voice messages that ask for personal or financial information.<br><br>2/. Links that lead to websites that look like legitimate pension providers but have subtle differences (e.g. misspellings in the domain name).<br><br>3/. Requests for payment or personal details in exchange for "free" pension reviews. | a/. Be wary of unsolicited emails or texts asking for personal or financial information.<br><br>b/. Always check the web address (URL) before entering any sensitive information online.<br><br>c/. As a minimum, enable two-factor authentication on your online pension accounts for added security.<br>d/. Regularly monitor your pension account for any suspicious activity. |

| **Pension Scams Targeting Vulnerable Individuals** | 1/. Preying on emotional vulnerability: Targeting individuals experiencing bereavement, divorce, or financial hardship<br><br>2/. Using misleading information: Exploiting individuals' lack of financial knowledge or understanding<br><br>3/. Pressuring individuals into making quick decisions: Creating | a/. Be vigilant and protect vulnerable individuals: If you know someone who may be at risk, offer support and guidance<br><br>b/. Report suspicious activity: Contact the FCA or the police if you suspect a scam<br><br>c/. Raise awareness: Educate yourself and others about common pension scams<br><br>d/. Seek professional help: Encourage vulnerable individuals to seek independent financial advice<br><br>e/. Trust your instincts: |
|---|---|---|

| | | |
|---|---|---|
| | a sense of urgency and fear of missing out<br><br>4/. Targeting specific demographics: Focusing on older individuals or those with limited English proficiency<br><br>5/. Operating outside of regulatory frameworks: Engaging in activities that are not authorized | If something feels wrong, it probably is. |
| **Social Media Scams** | 1/. Scammers contacting through social | a/. Be cautious of unexpected or unusual |

| | | |
|---|---|---|
| | media: using stolen or hijacked friends/family credentials<br><br>2/. Unusual request from friend/family for money not previously discussed<br><br>3/. WhatsApp impersonation text scammers posing as offsprings, or sometimes as friends or parents to ask for money urgently. | social media contact from friends/family<br><br>b/. Always verify by telephone with the family/friends whose details were used to contact you<br><br>c/. Verifying requests for money by contacting the supposed message sender directly via a known phone number, and to avoid transferring money to unfamiliar bank accounts. |
| **Pensions Transfer Scams** | 1/. Unregulated financial advice or companies offering | a/. Verify any pension transfer advice with a |

| | | |
|---|---|---|
| | pension transfers to "innovative" schemes<br><br>2/. Pressure to act quickly or make decisions under duress.<br><br>3/. Promises of high returns with little or no risk.<br><br>4/. Overly complex, 'by invitation only' Investment schemes that are difficult to understand | regulated financial adviser.<br><br>b/. Ensure that the adviser is on the Financial Conduct Authority (FCA) register.<br><br>c/. Be wary of investments that are hard to understand or involve significant fees.<br><br>d/. Always check that any transfer is to a legitimate and regulated pension scheme only |
| **Whisky Barrel Fraud & Scam** | 1/. **Whisky barrel fraud:** Scam conning victims to plough | a/. Do your due diligence before parting with a penny! Contact the warehouse where |

| | | |
|---|---|---|
| | their life savings and pensions into casks that were overpriced, don't exist, diluted to 40 **ABV (Alcohol By Volume)** or less or that have been sold to multiple "investors". | cask(s) are allegedly "stored" to validate: (i) the cask(s) unique ID exist (ii) content of the casks are minimum 63.5% **ABV** (iii) casks have not been sold to several "investors.<br><br>b/. Guaranteed annual returns on whiskey is a red flag. It's a long-term investment. |
| **Romance Grooming Scams** | 1/. **Online boyfriend scam:** Also known as romance grooming fraud, is when a criminal uses fake online profiles, identities and personas, to build romantic | a/. Be cautious when meeting new people online.<br><br>b/. Don't rush into a relationship and be sceptical of anyone pushing for a quick relationship or connection. |

| | | |
|---|---|---|
| | relationships with victims, then using that relationship and subtle emotional extortion to extract money or personal information.<br><br>2/. According to the BBC in England and Wales in 2020, there were 7,660 cases of romance fraud - up from 4,842 in 2019! | c/. Verify, Google information and be wary of inconsistencies in their stories.<br>d/. Don't send money or personal information to someone you haven't met in person. Never, ever!<br>e/. Talk to trusted friends and family about your online relationships.<br>f/. If you suspect you've been scammed, report it to the police or Action Fraud: 📞0300 123 2040 |
| **The Nigerian Prince or** | 1/. The Nigerian Prince scam is an | a/. Email or text messages usually contain |

| **Advance Fee Scam** | old but since evolved email phishing attack where fraudsters and scammers contact potential victims  typically by email or via text message and promise a large sum of money in return for some assistance with getting money out the country. Victims are usually asked to make an advance payment or share their personal financial details to get their reward. | a lot of grammatical mistakes.<br>b/. An email originates from a country you don't have any ties to or might have, as many 'Nigerian Prince' emails have been known to originate from Russia, China and the United States as well as Nigeria.<br>c/. You're promised money in exchange for carrying out a favour, but first you're asked to send money in advance from your bank or to reveal your personal data to ensure the victim is "genuine"!<br>d/. The scammer's sender's email address is |
|---|---|---|

| | | |
|---|---|---|
| | 2/. The Nigerian Prince scam is also known as advance fee fraud or 419 frauds, referring to the Nigerian Criminal Code section dealing with swindling.<br><br>3/. Finally, while this genre of online scam originally began in Nigeria, the fraud has evolved and many scammers using this fraudulent scheme are not Nigerians, therefore be on the lookout for phishing email | very long and may come from an unknown or unusual domain.<br><br>e/. The sender promises you an unrealistic amount of money for your assistance, usually for allowing the scammer to transfer money into your bank account. |

| | | |
|---|---|---|
| | addresses from other parts of the globe as well, especially USA, Russia, Romania, Albania and so forth. | |
| **Vishing** | 1/. **Vishing**—short for voice phishing—is a type of scam where fraudsters use phone calls or voice messages to trick people into revealing sensitive information like bank details, passwords, or personal identification numbers. | a/. Never share personal info over the phone unless you initiated the call and are sure of the identity of the recipient.<br>b/. Hang up and verify: If a call feels suspicious, hang up and call the official number of the organization held in your phone address book.<br>c/. Use call-blocking tools: Many smartphones and carriers offer features to block |

| | | |
|---|---|---|
| | 2/. Unlike email-based phishing, vishing relies on the human voice to create urgency or trust, often impersonating banks, government agencies, or tech support.<br><br>3/. Vishing uses three, key methods to breakthrough to victims as follows:-<br><br>3.1/. **Urgency & Fear Tactics:** Scammers might claim your bank account is | suspected spam or robocalls.<br>d/. Stay informed: Keep up to date with trends in financial scamming and fraud. And share the information among friends and family to increase awareness.<br>e/. Report it: In the UK, you can report vishing attempts to Action Fraud: 📞0300 123 2040 - or your bank's fraud alert number. |

| | | |
|---|---|---|
| | compromised or that you owe money to HMRC in the UK or IRS in America etc with threat of dire consequences if the victim didn't act quickly.<br><br>3.2/. **Voicemail Traps:** Typically, scammers leave alarming messages asking you to call back a number that takes you directly to the fraudsters or scammers.<br><br>3.3/. **Caller ID Spoofing**: Spoofing is one of the oldest scamming techniques | |

| | | |
|---|---|---|
| | where Scammers fake the caller ID to make it appear the call is from a trusted source or relative. | |

## Protecting Yourself Against Pension Fraud

Pension fraud remains a significant threat to pension holders, savers, and financial institutions. However, individuals can reduce their risk of falling victim to scams and fraudsters by staying vigilant and following online best practices, such as:

✅ Secure banking habits

✅ Cautious email and text message handling

✅ Exercising discretion when answering unsolicited telephone calls

Ideally, a person should seek professional, regulated financial advice before making any decisions regarding pension savings transfer, particularly when approached with an unsolicited offer.

The recommended default position in all cases involving pensions and financial transactions is scepticism.

✅ Be sceptical of any unsolicited offer.

✅ If a proposal sounds too good to be true, it probably is.

📞 **Reporting Pension Scams and Financial Fraud**

If you suspect you have been targeted by a pension scam, or have fallen victim to financial fraud, report it immediately to:

✔ The Financial Conduct Authority (FCA): 📞0800 111 6768

✔ Action Fraud: 📞0300 123 2040

✔ The Pensions Regulator: 📞0345 600 0707

✔ Your pension provider: 📞 (This was left intentionally blank!)

Additionally, **WhatsApp SMS voice notes and scam texts** can be forwarded to 📞 **7726**. The earlier an individual acts, the greater the likelihood of mitigating the financial and personal damage that may arise from fraud.

## Chapter

# 8 Pensions Information Discovery

If You Fail To Prepare You Must Be Prepared To Fail

## Teeing Up For Pension Purchase And Drawdown Success

Before starting the pension purchase process for an annuity or drawdown income, the Information Discovery Phase is where approximately 90% of the readiness-planning work is done.

To ensure a smooth application process, all tasks and activities in the Information Discovery Workplans and Work Instruction included below must be successfully completed—otherwise, a person's annuity or drawdown income application process will likely suffer costly financial delays.

Using **MoSCoW Prioritization Framework** for Pension Purchase During my Information Discovery phase, I used MoSCoW Prioritization Framework to nail down the vital information needed for pension purchase and drawdown. The advantage of MoSCoW is that it compels you to identify the information needed for the next stage of your purchase process and to have them to hand.

But this is easier said than done, because, unless the information required by the provider is prioritised and supplied, the purchase process will likely suffer delay.

**Figure 16.0 MoSCoW Prioritization Framework**

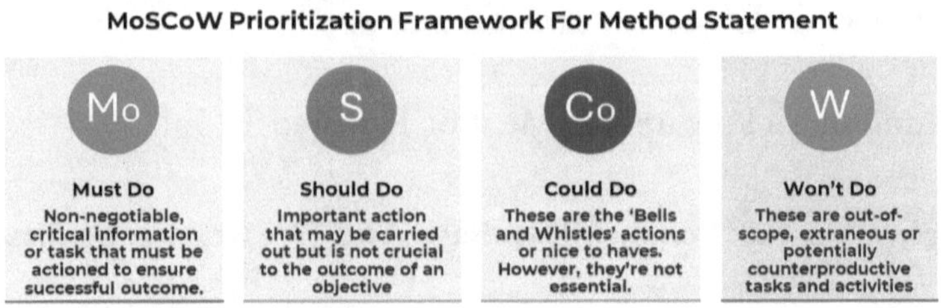


## The "Moment of Truth"

### Applying for Annuity Purchase & Drawdown Income

You're correct to assume that after saving diligently for nearly 40 years with a provider or providers, they would know who you were and grant access to your pension funds to allow you to enter drawdown or kick-off annuity purchase. While these assumptions are reasonable on the face of it and understandable, unfortunately, this is not how the pension application process works in real life.

Once an individual formally applies to access their pension pots, the provider's identity check and verification procedure moves into full gear, locking down the funds until ownership and entitlement are proven. The saver is then expected to go through a series of personal identification, verification, proof of address and so forth kicks in, because they can access their funds.

**The provider keeps the pot locked down until the claimant provides:**

✅ At least one UK Government-issued identification

✅ Pension scheme unique reference (scheme/contract no.) and documentation

✅ Additional verification documents requested by the provider

✅ Claimant's National Insurance number

The high incidence of financial fraud and scams targeting pensions makes strict security measures by providers an extremely high priority.

**Preparation For Pension Application (Workplan #3)**

In Workplan #3 on the next page, 10 SMART Objectives that must be completed before entering drawdown or buying annuity have been identified and collated.

These 10 objectives were subsequently broken down into deliverable tasks using a Work Instruction—these were the crucial, real-life, To-Do-List that I used during my pension purchase process. While the list might be different for different individuals if their circumstances are substantially different from mine, the list of ten objectives below is as good a place to start as any.

Workplan #3 and the Work Instruction were tested under fire and both templates proved extremely useful and highly effective.

If you bought this book, you're free to use the templates, subject to UK copyright laws and the terms below:-

📌 **Important Disclaimer**

❌ Using these templates does not guarantee success.

❌ Any use is entirely at your own discretion and risk.

❌ No warranties are made or implied.

**Workplan #3: SMART Objectives for Pension Purchase**

Workplan #3 below lists ten SMART Objectives which guided my pension purchase drawdown or annuity application processes.

Each SMART Objective represents a top-level activity, supported by a Work Instruction (WI), which is a work-breakdown document for Workplan #3. A Work Instruction is the same as a To-Do-List and is not unlike an IKEA instruction.

The purpose of the Work Instruction on the following page, developed from Workplan #3 below are as follows:-

✅ Secures maximum possible retirement income for the applicant

✅ Ensures the pension process is completed promptly

**Figure 17.0 Workplan #3 - SMART Objectives For Annuity/Drawdown**

| | |
|---|---|
| ☐ 1 | **National Insurance (NI) Top-Up** - Determine total qualifying years status for the full New State Pension. 🔗 Check Your NI Record<br><br>https://www.gov.uk/check-national-insurance-record |
| ☐ 2 | **Identity Harmonisation** - Harmonise personal and spouse identification information & reconcile relevant documentation such as utility bills etc. |
| ☐ 3 | **Locate Pension Pots & Online Enrolment** - Find and locate all pension pots and pension providers starting with: https://www.gov.uk/find-pension-contact-details |
| ☐ 4 | **Create Back-up Savings** - Create a ring-fenced savings to cover potential gaps between 'hard stop' retirement date and the commencement of monthly pension income. |

| | |
|---|---|
| ☐ 5 | ****Lifetime Allowance (LTA)** - Record LTA across all your pots as a percentage of total allowance. LTA tax year 2022-2023 was £1,073,100 (£1.07 million)<br><br>****No longer required since April 2024 but left in for completeness' sake.** |
| ☐ 6 | **NHS Medical Record** - Obtain yours and spouse's latest annual health-check vital statistics from GP surgery. This information is needed for the pension application process and some info must be GP surgery generated, especially when applying for Enhanced Annuity. |
| ☐ 7 | **Annuity/Drawdown Scratchpad** - Determine and collect mandatory information requirements for annuity/drawdown application interview |
| ☐ 8 | **Pension Assessment Interview (PAI)** - Determine the lead time from 'kick-off' of the PAI, to the start of annuity or drawdown income by asking the provider. Be warned, the lead time can be lengthy! |

| | |
|---|---|
| ☐ 9 | **Provider Effective Deadlines** - Align all provider deadlines to annuity start date and work backwards to determine when requested information and documents are due for submission to the provider. |
| ☐ 10 | **Pension Actuary Report** - The Actuary report should provide a 'lockdown date' for projected annuity award or commencement of income drawdown. |

**Work Instruction: Step-by-Step Guide for Pension Purchase**

The following Work Instruction (i.e. WI or To-Do-List)—numbered 001–010—is a step-by-step outline of the specific tasks that must be carried out to successfully deliver the ten SMART Objectives identified in Workplan #003 above.

The Work Instruction (WI) below is a true-to-life example of the information which I collected and used to kick-off my annuity purchase and drawdown process.

🚨 **Caution:** The To-Do-List or Work Instruction below was unique to my situation and is therefore not necessarily an exhaustive list.

**Figure 18.0 Work Instruction 001 - National Insurance or NI Top-Up**

| **Work Instruction 001 - National Insurance (NI) Top-Up** | |
|---|---|
| **Work Instruction No** | 001 |
| **Start and End Dates** | January 4th - January 10th (example date only!) |
| **Scope** | **National Insurance (NI) Top-Up** - To determine qualification status for full State Pension. If your National Insurance record started before April 2016, you will need 35 qualifying years to get the full rate of the new State Pension. |

| **Work Instruction**<br><br>**(To Do List)** | **Apply to HMRC for Govt. Gateway user ID** if you don't already have one. Otherwise use your login via the URL below.<br><br>🔗 https://www.access.service.gov.uk/login/signin/creds<br><br>The link takes you to the 'National Insurance' page, from there click the 'Check your national insurance contribution' link which takes you to 'Your National Insurance Records' page.<br><br>On 'Your National Insurance Records' page, you will see how many full years contributions you've made and how many 'Year Not In Full' contributions you have.<br><br>Based on your personal circumstances and current legislation, you may wish to 'top up' any gaps to increase your |
|---|---|

| | |
|---|---|
| | State Pension entitlement. You should take professional advice if you're unsure whether or not topping up is worth your while. Start with Pension Wise free on 📞0800 011 3797 or 🔗use our webchat<br><br>https://www.moneyhelper.org.uk/PensionsChat |

**Figure 19.0 - Work Instruction 002 - Identity (ID) Harmonisation**

| Work Instruction 002 - Identity (ID) Harmonisation | |
|---|---|
| **Work Instruction No** | 002 |
| **Start and End Dates** | Feb. 4 - Feb. 21 (example date only) |
| **Scope** | **Identity (ID) Harmonisation** - Harmonise personal & spouse |

| | |
|---|---|
| | identification information and to make ID data consistent across multiple documentation types such as:<br><br>(a) Passports (b) Driving Licences (3) Utility Bills (4) Electoral Register. |
| **Work Instruction**<br><br>**(To Do List)** | 1. **Valid Passports** -The pension applicant and spouse should hold valid UK passports as evidence of British citizenship or other acceptable ID verification.<br>2. **Driving Licence** - Both applicant and spouse should hold a valid driving licence. The address on both licences including post-codes, must be the same as the address held by the pension provider.<br>3. **Utility Bills** - The address on the utility bills must be the same as driving licence address and must |

be consistent with the address held by the provider.

4. **Utility Bills 2.0** - At least one of the utility bills must be in joint names if both lives are to be covered by the pension.
5. **Electoral Roll Record** - The applicant & spouse must ensure they're both on the Register for ID validation.
6. **National Insurance (NI) Number** - OK, I'm stating the blindingly obvious here, but your NI is the No.1 information all pension providers ask for. Please ensure your HMRC contact details match other IDs e.g. driving licence, utilities bills etc.

**Figure 20.0 Work Instruction 003 - Locate Pension Pots Enrol Online**

| Work Instruction 003 - Locate Pension Pots and Enrol Online | |
|---|---|
| **Work Instruction No** | 003 |
| **Start and End Dates** | March. 4 - March 31 (example date only) |
| **Scope** | **Locate Pension Pots & Enrol for Online Access** - Find & locate all pension pots and pension providers starting with 🔗 https://www.gov.uk/find-pension-contact-details |
| **Work Instruction (To Do List)** | **Locate Pension Pots** - Find and locate all pension pots and pension providers using the below online tool provided by the UK government. I used this tool to hunt for old pensions. 🔗 https://www.gov.uk/find-pension-contact-details |

| | |
|---|---|
| | **Pension Tracing Service** - Mon. to Fri. 10am to 3pm Telephone: 📞0800 731 0175 From outside the UK: 📞+44 (0)191 218 7777 Textphone: 📞0800 731 0176<br>**Relay UK** (if you cannot hear or speak on the phone): 📞18001 then 📞0800 731 0175 - Find out about call charges Monday to Friday, 10am to 3pm https://www.gov.uk/call-charges<br>**Enrol Online To Access Pension Your Pots** - All but one of my pension pots were moved online. I enrolled with all seven providers using the same email (user-name) but different passwords as a fraud prevention technique.<br>If a Past Employer is in Receivership or defunct - Use the Pension Protection Fund link below to access the Pension https://www.ppf.co.uk/sc search engine if your former employer has gone into receivership. |

**Figure 21.0 Work Instruction 004 - Back-Up Savings**

| Work Instruction 004 - Back-Up Savings | |
|---|---|
| **Work Instruction No** | 004 |
| **Start and End Dates** | April 1 - April 30 (example date only) |
| **Scope** | **Create Back-up Savings** - Create a ring-fenced savings to cover potential gaps between 'hard stop' retirement date and the start of monthly pension income or drawdown. |
| **Work Instruction (To Do List)** | **Create Back-up Savings** - Create a ring-fenced savings to cover potential gaps between 'hard stop' retirement date (i.e. last day of employment) and the start of monthly pension income or drawdown. I took a 'combination' approach, mixing and matching the options below to set-up my ring-fenced, back up savings intended to |

cover a potential 4-month gap. Now, as with the processes and approaches that I've discussed in this book, just because I created my backup savings using this method, doesn't mean you should too. But it is a starter for ten!

1. **Estimate the Gap Period:** I determined how long the gap might be between my retirement date and when my pension starts, taking into account any delays or unforeseen issues.
2. **Tax-Free Lump Sum:** 25% tax-free lump sum from two of my pension pots.
3. **Income Drawdown:** I kept two of my pension pots invested after drawdown and withdrew lump sums while the pots continued to grow. While this choice offered flexibility, I would come to regret taking this option because when I tried to annuitize the balance of my pot, my OMO providers declined *(I*

| | |
|---|---|
| | *will talk about what OMO is in a further chapter)* to pix-and-mix my drawdown pots with my uncrystallized (i.e. intact) pots. |

**Figure 22.0 Work Instruction 005 - LTA Allowance**

| **Work Instruction 005 - LTA Allowance** | |
|---|---|
| **Work Instruction No** | 005 |
| **Start and End Dates** | May 01 - May 31 (example date only) |
| **Scope** | **Lifetime Allowance (LTA)** - Record LTA usage across all your pots as a percentage of total allowance (100% for tax year 2022-2023 was £1,073,100 or £1.07 million) |

<table>
<tr>
<td>Work Instruction<br><br>(To Do List)</td>
<td>1. Contact all your pension providers (EXCEPT DWP) and ask them to provide you with the percentage of LTA equivalence for your pot.<br>2. When you've finished compiling your LTA allowances, your list should look like this, depending on the number of pension pots in your pension portfolio.<br>• 2.1 Pot #1 = 12% of LTA<br>• 2.2 Pot #2 = 9.7% of LTA<br>• 2.3 Pot #3 = 23.4% of LTA<br>• 2.4 Pot #4 = 15% of LTA etc<br><br>It's just as well that we don't have to provide LTA anymore, because getting LTA information from some providers was anything but straightforward. Although, the more efficient providers furnished me with this information without being asked!</td>
</tr>
</table>

**Figure 23.0 Work Instruction 006 - NHS Health Record**

| **Work Instruction 006 - NHS Health Record** | |
|---|---|
| **Work Instruction No** | 006 |
| **Start and End Dates** | June 6- June 6 (example date only) |
| **Scope** | **NHS Health Record** - Keep a record of yours and spouse's latest annual health-check vitals from GP surgery. This information is needed for the pension buying process and some info must be GP surgery generated. Date of readings (DoR) must be noted. |
| Work Instruction<br><br>(To Do List) | 1. Blood Pressure + (DoR)<br>2. Weight<br>3. Height<br>4. Medications<br>5. Impaired Life illnesses (may command Enhanced Annuity) |

An enhanced annuity is a type of pension that pays a higher income than a standard annuity. It's also known as an impaired life annuity or enhanced pension annuity. Enhanced annuity might pay anything between 10%-40% higher than a standard annuity.

**How does Enhanced Annuity work?**

- An enhanced annuity pays more because of your health history or current health.
- The higher income is based on the expectation that your health could shorten your life.
- You could qualify if you have certain impaired life conditions, a lifestyle or illness that could shorten your life. e.g.
    - Having Type 2 diabetes
    - High blood pressure
    - Being overweight
    - Having a history of stroke, cancer, heart attack, kidney failure, chronic asthma, or multiple sclerosis

**Figure 24.0 Work Instruction 007 - Annuity or Drawdown Scratchpad**

<table>
<tr><th colspan="3">1/2 - Work Instruction 007 - Annuity/Drawdown Scratchpad</th></tr>
<tr><td>Work Instruction No</td><td colspan="2">007</td></tr>
<tr><td>Start and End Dates</td><td colspan="2">July 4 - July 14 (example date only)</td></tr>
<tr><td>Scope</td><td colspan="2">Annuity Application Scratchpad - Preparatory notes intended to assist with:- (a) Annuity and Drawdown telephone interview (b) Drawdown and Annuity Form filling.</td></tr>
<tr><td rowspan="2">Work Instruction<br><br>(To Do List)</td><td>Preparatory Information</td><td>Applicant's Response</td></tr>
<tr><td>1. National Insurance (NI) Number</td><td></td></tr>
</table>

| Annuity/Drawdown Checklist | | |
|---|---|---|
| | 2. Pension Provider(s) | |
| | 3. Pension Fund Current Value | |
| | 4. Pension Policy Number(s) | |
| | 5. Is Pension In Drawdown or has 25% tax-free lump sum been withdrawn? | |
| | 6. Is 25% Tax-Free Lump Sum required from this pension pot? | |

| | | |
|---|---|---|
| | 7. Is Pension policy a Defined Contribution scheme? | |
| | **2/2 - Work Instruction** | |
| | **Preparatory Information** | **Applicant's Response** |
| | 8. Is Pension policy Defined Benefits? | |
| | 9. Is Policy a Stakeholder Pension? | |
| | 10. Is It a Single Life Annuity Pension? | |

| | | |
|---|---|---|
| | 11. **Is it a Joint Life Annuity Pension?**<br><br>If Joint pension, what's the preferred percentage split between You/Spouse?<br><br>• **You / Spouse**<br>• 50 / 50%<br>• 60 / 40%<br>• 70 / 30%<br>• 80 / 20%<br>• 90 / 10% | |
| | 12. **Drawdown Designation**: You'll need to declare the portion of your pension you want to use for drawdown. | |

| | | |
|---|---|---|
| | 13. **Drawdown Investment Choices:** You'll need to choose how you want to invest the remaining part of your pension pot after taking your tax-free lump sum. | |
| | 14. **Drawdown Tax-Free Lump Sum Choice:** You'll decide whether you want to take your tax-free lump sum all at once or in installments. | |

| | | |
|---|---|---|
| | 15. What's your planned retirement date? | |
| | 16. What medications are you currently taking? | |
| | 17. If you're a smoker, how many cigarettes do you smoke daily? | |
| | 18. What's your height and weight? | |
| | 19. What's your spouse's height and weight? | |

| | | |
|---|---|---|
| | 20. Please list any medical conditions for which you're currently taking medications and list the year treatment began. | |
| | 21. Please list any medical conditions for which your spouse is currently taking medications and list the year treatment began. | |
| | 22. Please list any prescribed medications you're taking with dosage and state which year | |

|  |  |  |
|---|---|---|
|  | you started these medications. |  |
|  | 23. Please list any prescribed medications your spouse is taking with dosage and state which year these medications were started. |  |

**Annuity Buying & Income Drawdown Meeting Is Good To Go**

Assuming all preliminary activities captured in Workplan #3 and the To-Do-List or Work Instruction 007 above have been completed, the annuity pension purchase or income drawdown interview which could last up to two hours, should proceed smoothly. Depending on personal circumstances, the provider might request additional information and data beyond what was outlined in the preceding Workplan and Work Instruction.

Although, in over 95% of cases, the information provided in Work Instructions #01 to #07 should be sufficient to address the provider's potential questions.

Without the information prepared in advance, there's a strong likelihood that a significant amount of time could be lost as the provider's Actuary may not progress an individual's pension applications until all information is provided.

## Chapter

# 9 Buying Annuity Or Drawing Income

In For A Penny In For A Pound

## The Public/Private Pension Pillars

**The three central pillars of retirement pensions are:**

1 Relevant legislation governing pensions

2 Pension providers responsible for managing pension schemes.

3 The Pension Ombudsman, which handles complaints, disputes, and oversees the Pension Protection Fund.

**Figure 25.0 The Pensions Pillars**

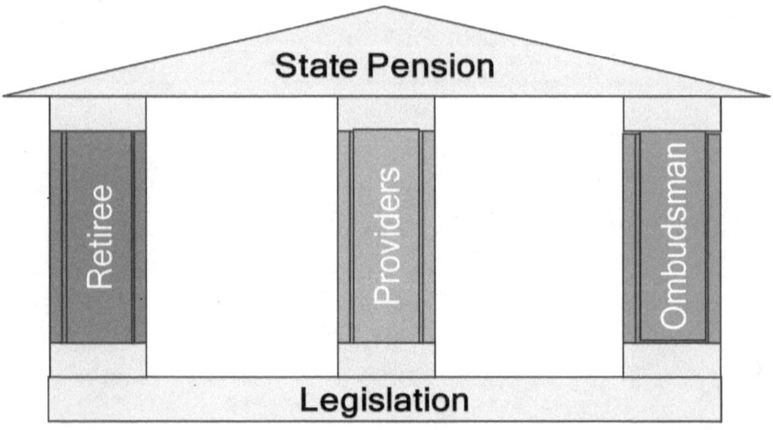

## Pension Income Options: Drawdown or Annuities

The first time most people realise saving for a pension is not the same as buying a pension or drawdown income, is when they formally approach the provider to kick-off their pension arrangements.

It is usually at this point in the pension-buying process that people realize there's a financial plot twist—that pensions are like German sentences—the meaning comes right at the end!

In earlier chapters, I briefly discussed income drawdown and annuities. In this chapter, I will explore both options in greater detail, as they represent the two primary pension income choices available upon retirement. Although a third option exists—taking a lump sum payment—this is largely self-explanatory, so it will not be covered in any detail.

## Deciding on Your Pension Income Preferences

### Choosing between income drawdown, annuities or a Combo:

1 Tax implications

2 Serious financial risks, such as running out of money in later life

3 In the case of annuities, once an annuity is purchased, it's an irreversible decision. This means an individual or couple cannot change their mind, cash it in, or transfer it to another provider at a later date.

📌The following analysis is purely informational and educational. It is not a substitute for professional financial advice.

Given the complexities of retirement income choices, it's highly advisable to seek financial guidance before selecting an annuity, drawdown, or a combination of both.

In my personal case, after careful consideration and following consultations with several financial experts, I chose an annuity and income drawdown Combo.

However, just because this worked for me doesn't mean it's right for everyone.

Your decision should be based on your unique financial situation, risk appetite, and ideally, informed by a professional financial adviser.

## UK Pension Preferences: Drawdown vs. Annuities

According to recent Financial Conduct Authority (FCA) data, a significantly smaller percentage of UK pensions are used to purchase annuities, with the majority of retirees opting for drawdown instead.

📌**Recent figures indicate:**

✔ Only 22% of pension pots are used to purchase annuities.

✔ The remaining 78% of retirees choose income drawdown.

**What Is an Annuity?**

In general terms, an annuity is a regular income contract that converts pension savings into a stable annual income, which is paid:

✔ Monthly

✔ Quarterly

✔ Biannually

✔ Annually

📌 **An annuity provides:**
✔ A guaranteed income for life, or
✔ Income for a specified period

**It's common for retirees to purchase an annuity using either:**

- A portion of their pension pot (mixed with the 25% tax-free lump sum)
- The entirety of their pension savings

**Types of Annuities in the UK**

There are many types of annuities, including fixed-term, lifetime, and investment-linked annuities.

**Here are the most popular annuity options:**

📌 **Fixed-Term Annuity**

✔ Provides a regular income for a set period, typically between 1 and 20 years.

📌 **Lifetime Annuity**

✔ Pays an income for the rest of the retiree's life, based on life expectancy.

📌 **Investment-Linked Annuity**

✔ Similar to a lifetime annuity, but income varies each year and is not guaranteed.

📌 **Enhanced Annuity**

✔ Offers higher payouts for retirees with medical conditions or unhealthy lifestyles.

📌 **Single Life Annuity**

✔ Converts a pot into a guaranteed income for the remainder of the retiree's life.

📌 **Joint Life Annuity**

✔ Pays a guaranteed income while the retiree and their spouse are alive.

📌 **Escalating Annuity**

✔ Starts with lower initial payments, but income gradually increases each year.

📌 **Deferred Annuity**

✔ Funds remain untouched until an agreed-upon future date.

📌 **Inflation-Linked Annuity**

✔ Increases annually in line with the Retail Price Index (RPI).

📌 **Annuity Value Protection**

✔ Allows retirees to protect a portion of the money spent on their annuity.

## The Open Market Option (OMO) - Annuity Pension

OMO was introduced as part of the 1975 United Kingdom Finance Act and was designed to allow individuals to shop around for a better pension annuity rather than being restricted to their original or existing pension provider.

OMO has proven to be an indispensable and game-changing piece of legislation, putting hundreds of millions of pounds into retirees' pockets and transforming the annuity market.

**How OMO Revolutionized Pension Annuities**

Before OMO, research suggested that the average retiree lost around £13,000 over 20 years by not shopping around to secure the most competitive annuity available.

OMO changed all that—provided retirees took advantage of it. Since its inception, the market competition created by OMO has ensured that individuals purchasing pension annuities can shop around for the best deals.

However, despite its clear advantages, many people approaching retirement remain unaware of this provision. Fortunately for me—driven by investigative curiosity and meticulous planning—I discovered OMO and successfully took advantage of it to maximize my pension income.

🚨 **A crucial fact to remember:**

Unless an individual's pension pot is converted into an annuity through the OMO process (*assuming that's their preference*), they are in all probability, not securing the best retirement income for their savings.

Additionally, it's worth remembering that when purchasing an annuity, you are locked in for life—with no exit pathway!

📌 This makes it absolutely essential for an individual to explore and understand their OMO options, before committing themselves to an annuity contract.

**Enhanced Annuities: A Hidden OMO Benefit**

Another key advantage of OMO that many retirees overlook is the Enhanced Annuity.

✔ This is a boosted annuity that provides a higher income based on factors such as health conditions and lifestyle choices.

✔ Retirees suffering from certain medical conditions may qualify for an Enhanced Annuity, thus increasing their pension income.

Despite these benefits, many people approaching retirement fail to utilize OMO.

Several reasons have been cited for lack of OMO adoption, including:

- Lack of awareness or knowledge gap
- Complexity associated with transferring funds to an OMO annuity
- Penalties imposed by some pension providers for transferring to OMO
- Older pension schemes that do not allow OMO

- Additional administrative steps that retirees may prefer to avoid
- A simpler pension application process without OMO

**The Financial Consequences of Ignoring OMO Process**

Crucially, making the wrong decision about retirement pension could cost an individual, tens of thousands of pounds over their lifetime.

📌 Consequently, it's vital to seek professional financial advice regarding OMO and other pension options before retirement, as annuities represent a lifetime financial commitment—with no exit strategy.

During my annuity application process, I was astonished by the huge variation in the annuity offers I received.

✔ The difference between the highest and lowest offers ranged from 18%–33%.
✔ Over a 20-year retirement period, in my case alone—this translated to over £200,000 in lost income.

**But you might be wondering:**

📌 If OMO makes such a significant difference to annuity offers, why aren't pension providers legally compelled to provide it?

Indeed, under the Pensions Act 2014, providers are legally obliged to remind pension savers they can shop around using OMO to secure a better annuity—provided their pension scheme allows it.

However, legal obligation, practical implementation, and enforcement are three different things. Therefore, just because a provider is legally obliged to inform pension savers about OMO doesn't mean they will.

**This is why it's essential for anyone approaching retirement to:**

✔ Familiarize themselves with pension benefits and entitlements.

✔ Understand the Open Market Option and its advantages.

✔ If necessary, consult with a regulated financial adviser. Otherwise, the potential financial consequences could be significant.

**What's an Income Drawdown Pension?**

Income drawdown—also simply known as 'drawdown' or flexible retirement income—allows individuals to access their pension savings while keeping the remainder invested in stocks, property, or other assets.

📌 **How Income Drawdown Works:**

✔ You withdraw a portion of your pension savings as income.

✔ The remaining funds stay invested, giving potential for growth—but also risk of value depreciation.

✔ A drawdown pot remains at risk if invested.

A prime example of drawdown risk was the recent decline in stocks and shares, following Donald Trump's imposition of global tariffs, which negatively impacted investment-based pensions globally. As I previously stated in earlier chapters, worldwide stock markets lost an estimated U.S. $5.8 trillion (e.g. S&P 500 companies etc).

📌**Key Aspects of Drawdown**

✔ **Tax-Free Lump Sum**

You can generally take up to 25% of your pension pot as a tax-free lump sum (*subject to legal maximums*).

✔ **Income Withdrawals**

The remaining 75% stays invested, and you can withdraw funds as needed—however, withdrawals are subject to income tax.

✔ **Investment Growth**

The remaining funds in your pension pot continue to be invested, with potential for growth or loss, depending on market performance.

### Types of Drawdown

📌 **Flexi-Access Drawdown**

✔ The most common type, allowing retirees to withdraw income as needed.

📌 **Capped Drawdown**

✔ Available only to individuals who started drawdown before April 6, 2015.

**Figure 26.0 Table Comparing Pension Drawdown & Annuities**

| Feature | Pension Drawdown | Annuities |
|---|---|---|
| **Flexibility** | High - You can choose how much and when to withdraw | Low - Fixed income, predetermined value |
| **Investment Growth** | Potential for growth, but carries investment risk | No growth, fixed income, unless index linked etc |

| | | |
|---|---|---|
| **Income Certainty** | Variable income, dependent on investment performance | Guaranteed income, predictable and stable. |
| **Income Tax** | Up to 25% tax-free lump sum, income withdrawal taxed as income | Up to 25% tax-free lump sum, annuity payments taxed as income |
| **Management Required** | On-going management and fees | No. Not required |
| **Death Benefit** | Remaining funds can be inherited | Option available for spouse or partner income continuation |
| **Risks** | Market and longevity risks | No market risk, but inflation can erode purchasing power |

In the end, whichever choice of pension income an individual makes, it's important to consider independent financial advice to ensure the choice is the right one for that person. Pension income decisions rarely offer a second bite of the cherry!

## The U.K. State Pension

The Department for Work and Pensions (DWP) has been the brunt of considerable criticism over the past 14 years (2010-2024), largely due to its internal culture, institutional practices and its role at the sharp end of various Tory government austerity policies.

However, when it comes to the State Pension, the DWP stands out as an exemplar, surpassing most private pension providers in efficiency and competence—at least that was my personal experience.

Assuming a person has all their paperwork in order, the DWP delivers a frictionless, world-class pension service—worthy of commendation.

But don't just take my word for it. Let's explore the intricacies of how the U.K's State Pension system works.

The amount of State Pension a person receives is determined by the number of years they paid National Insurance (NI)—this is known as qualifying years.

At present, a full new State Pension requires 35 years of NI contributions or credits. Those with at least 10 years receive a proportionate amount, while those with less than 10 years do not qualify for State Pension payments.

However, retirees with fewer than 10 years of contributions may be eligible for Pension Credit, a means-tested benefit for individuals over State Pension age on low incomes.

📌**Pension Credit**

To contact Pension Credit please call them on: 📞0800 99 1234.

**Figure 27.0 Check Your State Pension Forecast**

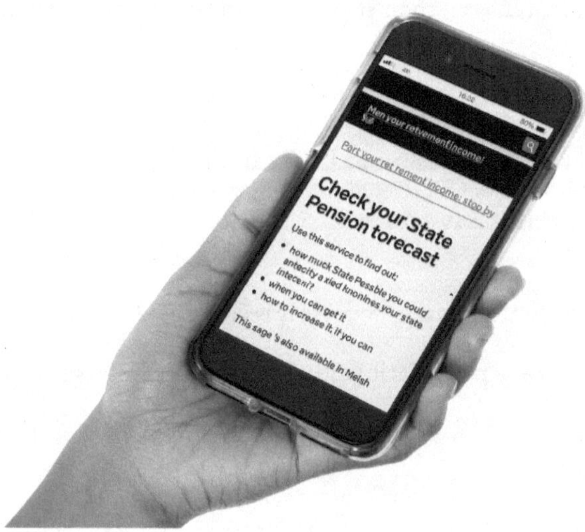

## State Pension Amount And The Triple Lock System

**The full State Pension is currently worth:**

✔ £11,973 per year, or

✔ £230.25 per week

This amount increases annually according to the 'triple lock' mechanism, which guarantees pension increases based on the highest of these three factors:

✅ Inflation or Consumer Price Index or CPI.

✅ Average wage growth.

✅ A fixed minimum of 2%

🚨 **Potential Future Uncertainty:**

As of January 2025, reports suggest the Triple Lock commitment could be revised or reduced in the future. However, this currently appears to be pure speculation since the Labour government has neither confirmed nor denied it.

Regardless, given this potential uncertainty, it's best not to assume the system will remain unchanged indefinitely.

## Checking Your National Insurance (NI) Record

📌 **Key Requirements:**

✔ To qualify for the new State Pension, you usually need at least 10 qualifying years on your NI record.

✔ The actual amount you receive depends on the number of qualifying years you have accumulated.

📌 **Ways to Qualify for the State Pension:**

✔ By working and paying NI contributions.

✔ By receiving NI credits (*e.g. during periods of unemployment or caring for dependents*).

✔ By paying voluntary NI contributions

📌 **Check Your NI Record:**

🔗UK Government Digital Gateway:

🔗https://www.gov.uk/check-national-insurance-record

🔗Check your NI record and obtain a State Pension forecast at: Gov.uk website https://www.gov.uk/check-national-insurance-record or use the DWP mobile app, which:

✔ Displays your State Pension age.

✔ Estimate how much you can expect to receive.

✔ Identifies ways to increase your qualifying years (e.g. voluntary contributions)

📌 **Important:**

🚨 Please note that opportunities to increase qualifying years are often time-sensitive, with strict deadlines. Consequently, it's important to act with urgency whenever the chance arises to top-up NI contributions.

**Eligibility Based on NI Contributions**

✔ If you have 35 years of NI contributions, you may receive the full State Pension. I said may because of the 35-year SERPS qualification trap described **below.

✔ If you have between 10 and 34 years, you will receive a proportion of the full amount.

✔ If you have less than 10 years, you are not usually eligible for the State Pension.

🚨 **Additional Considerations:**

✔ If you were contracted out before April 6, 2016, you may receive less than the full amount.

✔ If you claim the new State Pension and have a low income, you may be eligible for Pension Credit.

🚨**The 35-Year SERPS Qualification Trap

The introduction of the New State Pension (April 2016) and the previous State Earnings-Related Pension Scheme (SERPS) can negatively impact an individual's ability to qualify for the full 35-year State Pension, even if they technically have 35 years of NI contributions or more.

This is because NI was collected at a lower rate for those contracted out of SERPS compared to individuals that didn't.

📌 **How Contracting Out (SERPS) Can Impact Your Pension:**

**1. Impact of Contracting Out**

✔ Individuals who were contracted out of SERPS—or part of a contracted-out workplace pension—may not have built up the full additional State Pension under the old system.

✔ This can result in a lower 'starting amount' when calculating their New State Pension, potentially requiring additional years of NI contributions to reach the full rate.

**2. New State Pension Calculation**

✔ The New State Pension is calculated at a flat rate, and any previous SERPS entitlement is factored into a 'starting amount'.

✔ If a pension saver's starting amount is lower than the full New State Pension rate, they must continue contributing to NI to reach full entitlement.

**Applying for a State Pension *vs* Workplace/Private Pension**

📌 **The State Pension Claim Process**

Getting the State Pension is relatively straightforward however it is not an automatic benefit, you must make a formal claim for it as follows:-

✅ When you reach the State Pension age, currently 66 for both men and women and increasing to 67 in monthly increments from May 2026, you'll receive a letter of invitation from the Pension Service (Department for Work and Pensions - DWP) to claim your State Pension.

✅ The key word here is "claim"—the State pension is not automatic; it is a contributory benefit and must be claimed or applied for by the retiree.

To claim your pension, visit the official government portal through this link: 📌🔗 **Apply for Your State Pension Here**

**https://www.gov.uk/get-state-pension/**

Once on the webpage, follow the instructions, and Bob's your uncle! As long as you meet all criteria, the process should be smooth and efficient. The DWP Pension Service is highly competent, so unless you're extremely unlucky, claiming the State Pension is a relatively straightforward process.

**Understanding The Lifetime Allowance (LTA) Changes**

The first thing to say about LTA is that as of April 6, 2024, the LTA was abolished! However, many pension laws remain unchanged, including following:-

✔ The annual allowance limit, currently £60,000, remains in place.

✔ If a person's combined pension pots totalled £2 million, their 25% tax-free lump sum is still capped at £268,275.00.

📌 **Example:**
An individual cannot claim 25% of £2 million (£500,000)—due to the cap of £268,275.00.

Since pension regulations remain complex, I strongly recommend seeking professional financial advice to navigate these rules effectively.

## Configuring Your Retirement Income

**Retirement income is not one-size-fits-all.**

The typical retirement income package consists of three streams:

✔ 25% tax-free lump sum (capped at £268,275.00 for the 2025/2026 tax year)

✔ Annuity payments

✔ Drawdown income

Each option has its own benefits and risks, making financial advice crucial.

## Making Your Pension Application

Your pension arrangements at retirement are arguably one of the most important financial decisions of your life after cessation of employment.

Any choice an individual makes will impact them for the rest of their natural life, which could span 30 years or more.

Regardless of how often a person has heard it repeated that pension purchases are complex, it's essential to enter the process with a solid understanding of your options and the potential long-term consequences.

A good learner driver would not apply to take a driving test until they knew the Highway Code as the test would otherwise be a failure and a pointless exercise.

And so, it should be with a pension buying application. Knowing one's pension options at the most basic level is critical to making informed decisions, on a crucial financial matter that will last a lifetime.

## Applying for State Pension

I started my 'pension retirement pursuit' by applying first for my State Pension. It was relatively pain free and straightforward since I

had the following:

✔ DWP letter of invitation and my unique invitation code.

✔ NI number

✔ U.K. government issued ID (Passport in my case)

✔ Other proof of identity

## Key Pension Application Considerations

**SMART** Objectives (Workplan #4 below) and Work Instruction (To-Do-List) for both private and State pension applications outline the tasks and activities to be carried out as follows:-

**Each item is accompanied by a Work Instruction, detailing:**

✔ Key actions required

✔ Lessons learned from my own application process

**Figure 28.0 Workplan #4 - Buying Annuity or Entering Drawdown**

| | | |
|---|---|---|
| ☐ | **1** | **'Wake-Up Packs'** - Request from pension provider(s) and follow directions. |
| ☐ | **2** | **State Pension** - Check your NI eligibility and apply for your State Pension |
| ☐ | **3** | **Annuity Assessment Interview** - 'Kick-off' to annuity purchase process |
| ☐ | **4** | **Provider OMO Report** - Obtain OMO quotes and review to inform choice |
| ☐ | **5** | **Letter of Authority (LoA)** - Complete LoA for each pension pot transfer to preferred annuity provider |

**Figure 29.0 Workplan Instruction 008 - Request 'Wake-Up Packs'**

| Work Instruction 008 - Request 'Wake-Up Packs' | |
|---|---|
| **Work Instruction No** | 008 |
| **Start and End Dates** | May 01 - May 31 (example only) |
| **Scope** | **'Wake-Up Packs' (WUP)** - Request WUP from provider(s) |
| **Work Instruction**<br><br>**(To Do List)** | 1. No less than 6 months from the date an individual expects retirement income to begin, they should contact their pension providers (EXCEPT DWP) and ask them to provide them with a 'Wake-Up' Pack.<br>2. The pack contains the latest pension statements, pension options, providers application |

process and the information the provider wants from the applicant.

3. When the 'Wake-Up' pack is received, the individual should read it thoroughly, especially the part relating to pension options and the information required by the provider to support annuity or drawdown application. It is advisable to call the provider if an individual is unclear about anything in the pack.
4. Alternatively, an individual may call Pension Wise for advice on their options or other questions. Pension Wise can be reached via this number: 📞0800 731 0469 and it was free at the time of writing this book.

**Figure 30.0 Work Instruction 009 - UK State Pension: Check NI**

| Work Instruction 009 - Check NI eligibility & apply for the State Pension | |
|---|---|
| **Work Instruction No** | 009 |
| **Start and End Dates** | May 01 - May 31 (example only) |
| **Scope** | **State Pension Application** - Check NI eligibility and apply for the State Pension |
| **Work Instruction**<br><br>**(To Do List)** | 1. Check NI records for your eligibility for State Pension.<br><br>2. If an individual is eligible (minimum 10 years NI contribution), they should call DWP Pension Office Tel: 📞0800 169 0154 or 📞0800 587 0892 for N. Ireland. Postal application allowed. |

| | |
|---|---|
| | 3. DWP requires the following information when a person calls: Personal Invitation code sent by DWP Pension Service inviting the individual to apply for the State Pension. If a person hasn't received an invitation code, they should apply for an invitation code using the link below, providing they're within 3 months of reaching State Pension age. 🔗 https://get-state-pension.service.gov.uk/request-invitation-code<br><br>• Bank or building society account details.<br>• Date of your most recent marriage, civil partnership or divorce<br>• Dates of any time spent living or working abroad<br>• The date from which you want your retirement pension paid. |

| | |
|---|---|
| | 4. Once an individual has applied, they'll receive a letter from the Department for Work and Pensions (DWP) informing them of the pension amount they'll receive. This information should be kept as it might be needed for annual tax returns.<br><br>5. The Pension Service must be notified if an individual's personal circumstances have changed. |

**Figure 31.0 Work Instruction 010 - Annuity/Drawdown Interview**

| Work Instruction 010 - Annuity/Drawdown Interview | |
|---|---|
| **Work Instruction No** | 010 |
| **Start and End Dates** | June 01 - July 05 (example only) |

| Scope | **Annuity/Drawdown Pension Assessment Interview** - 'Kick-off' annuity application process |
| --- | --- |
| **Work Instruction**<br><br>**(To Do List)** | 1. At least 12=16 Weeks from the date you wish your annuity to begin, you should call your pension provider and ask for an 'Annuity Assessment Interview' with their nominated annuity broker. Typical lead time from your request to interview appointment date is 4-5 weeks.<br><br>2. On the day of the interview appointment, please take with you Work Instruction 007 - Annuity & Drawdown Application Scratchpad with you as aide-mémoire. It will help you |

| | |
|---|---|
| | answer many of the questions asked during the interview.<br><br>3. The provider interviewer will record your answers on the master copy of the annuity application form at their end.<br><br>4. The provider will forward the original form completed over the phone to you to do as below:<br><br>(a) review information provided<br><br>(b) provide additional or any missing information as necessary<br><br>(c) add "wet" signature (i.e. handwritten signature)<br><br>5. Return the signed form preferably by Signed For Postage with any original copies of specified personal identification |

| | |
|---|---|
| | and medical report/information within 24-48 hours of receipt.<br><br>6. Pension providers routinely contact General Practice doctors to confirm any health-related information or data provided. This is more likely where Enhanced Annuity was offered to you, consequently, please ensure your medical information is accurate because the pension provider could legally reduce your annuity if the health information or data you provided are not aligned to the information held by your GP surgery or doctor. |

**Figure 32.0 Work Instruction 011 - Actuary OMO Report (Annuity)**

| Work Instruction 011 - Actuary OMO Report (Annuity Pension) | |
|---|---|
| **Work Instruction No** | 011 |
| **Start and End Dates** | June 01 - July 05 (example only) |
| **Scope** | **Pension Actuary OMO Report** - Obtain provider OMO quotes and review to inform choice of OMO annuity |
| **Work Instruction**<br><br>**(To Do List)** | 1. This Work Instruction applies if a person is transferring their pension pot to another provider to take advantage of the Open Market Option or OMO for annuity.<br><br>2. The retirement broker nominated by the person's provider should, after the |

| | |
|---|---|
| | telephone interview in Work Instruction 010 - (Annuity Pension Assessment Interview), provide in writing the range of OMO annuity rates advised by various pension providers competing for an individual's pension pot.<br><br>3. Review your annuity proposals and offers as appropriate and take professional advice if you must, before deciding which OMO offer you wish to accept as pension income.<br><br>4. You should notify the provider (OMO broker) in writing, which annuity company/offer you wish to accept.<br><br>5. Once the Working Instruction 010 - Annuity Pension Assessment Interview form is completed, submitted and an annuity income option is chosen, the retiree should clarify the timelines the provider is working to and how these |

| | |
|---|---|
| | milestones align to their preferred annuity start date.<br><br>6. Ideally, the retiree should ask the provider to confirm these timelines in writing, failing that, the retiree should note the timelines agreed to during conversation with the provider and confirm these back in writing, asking the provider "to correct estimated timelines if they're unrealistic, incorrect or unfeasible".<br><br>7. The above step is important to ensure both retiree and the OMO broker are on the same page in regard to timelines and milestones. Serious deviation from these timelines by the broker may be good grounds for a claim at a future date, were things to go 'South'. |

**Figure 33.0 Work Instruction 012 - Letter of Authority (LoA)**

| Work Instruction 012 - Letter of Authority (LoA) | |
|---|---|
| **Work Instruction No** | 012 |
| **Start and End Dates** | June 01 - July 05 (example only) |
| **Scope** | **Letter of Authority (LoA)** - Complete LoA for each pension pot transfer to annuity provider.<br><br>1. This Work Instruction applies if a retiree is transferring their pension pot to another provider, to take advantage of the Open Market Option or OMO. |
| **Work Instruction**<br><br>**(To Do List)** | 2. The retiree must complete and sign a 'Letter of Authority', instructing the retiree's ORIGINAL pension holder, to transfer or release their pot to an OMO annuity broker or different provider. |

| | |
|---|---|
| | 3. The final decision whether a retiree's transferred pot is accepted rests with the chosen provider.<br><br>4. The retiree must be aware that if their transferred pot is refused, it is the retiree's responsibility to manage the return of the pot to their original provider.<br><br>5. Please note that a transferred fund may be rejected by the OMO annuity provider for a variety of reasons e.g. (a) the pot was in drawdown (b) a 25% tax-free lump sum was withdrawn (c) the retiree mistakenly tried to mix-and-match defined contribution (DC) with a defined benefit (DB) pot.<br><br>6. The retiree must be aware that if their pot is rejected after transferring and is then returned to the original provider, it |

would in all likelihood be returned into a new Scheme because the old account would have been closed immediately after the transfer.

Consequently, when the pot is returned, it would most likely be sent to a newly opened Stakeholder or private pension account. In that case, it is the responsibility of the retiree to ensure the re-transferred pot into a new account is timely and successful. This exact situation happened to me, and I found out the hard way that many pension providers have very poor administrative systems to manage exceptions. A retiree ignores this warning at their peril!

**Pension Income Choices: Annuity *versus* Drawdown**

📌 **Flexibility**

✔ Pension drawdown offers greater control over income and investments, making it the more flexible option.

✔ Annuities provide predictability and a fixed income but offer less flexibility.

📌 **Income Certainty**

✔ Annuities guarantee a regular and steady income, which helps with budgeting.

✔ Pension drawdown income varies based on investment performance.

📌 **Investment Growth**

✔ Drawdown allows pension funds to continue growing but comes with investment risk.

✔ Annuities do not typically offer growth, unless inflation-linked or indexed, but provide stability.

📌 **Management and Fees**

✔ Drawdown requires ongoing management, often incurring fees.

✔ Annuities require no management and have no overhead costs.

📌 **Risk**

✔ Drawdown carries market and longevity risks, meaning the pension pot may deplete too soon.

✔ Annuities protect against market risks but may fail to keep up with inflation unless indexed at the outset.

## Navigating Pension Income Options

By understanding their pension income choices either through acquired knowledge and advice—including the Open Market Option (OMO)—a retiree can make informed decisions to maximize their pension income in retirement.

Furthermore, by sticking to clear pension application timelines, a retiree can manage the complex transition into retirement with confidence. Because as the saying goes: "You've done your homework, got the tee-shirt and earned your secure retirement!"

## Chapter

# 10 Monitoring And Intervention

Don't Make A Promise Unless You Intend To Keep It

## What You Don't Measure You Can't Manage Or Improve

You'll recall in the previous chapter on planning and preparation, that I made several references to timelines, deadlines, and milestones—that is, a fixed date by which an activity must be concluded or the output of a task completed.

**Timelines, deadlines, and milestones are critical because they:**

✔ Measure progress on planned activities.

✔ Determine whether tasks are on track or completed on time and to a satisfactory standard.

✔ Dependencies—tasks that must be completed before another begins or ends.

In some cases, tasks have no dependencies and can proceed in parallel with others, although both may need to be completed before the final output is considered delivered.

For the uninitiated, managing these interconnected and independent activities can sometimes feel like juggling hot potatoes while on stilts!

This is why collecting a variety of information as the annuity or drawdown application progresses is absolutely vital.

**The information gathered will prove invaluable for:**

✅ Early detection of issues and risks with pension applications

✅ Chasing inevitable delays.

✅ Estimating when to schedule follow on activities or tasks

✅ Judging when work-in-progress tasks and activities will be completed

✅ Intervening to correct issues when a pension provider's output goes off track.

✅ Timely identification of potential issues or deviations from planned schedule.

✅ Ensuring planned pension objectives are completed on time

**Figure 34.0 Example Of A High Level Timeline and Milestones**

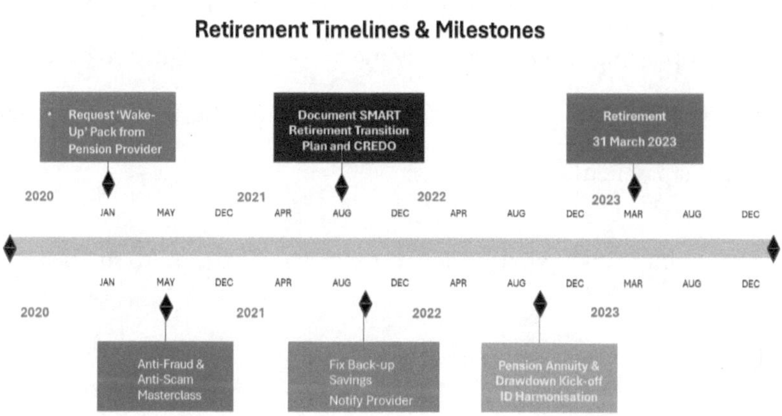

## Monitoring Your Pension Income Application

To monitor an activity or task, such as an annuity or drawdown application, means keeping it under constant review while measuring its progress against pre-determined timeline targets (i.e. milestones).

It's also essential to keep records of significant progress details, such as excessive delays or other unexpected issues.

### The Importance of Monitoring Pension Application Progress

Let me set the stage. Monitoring a pension application's progress on a weekly to fortnightly basis is critical to ensuring the first pension income arrives on time.

Furthermore, every week a pension income is delayed, it creates a financial gap that needs to be covered using personal savings or loans.

Earlier in this book, you may recall that one of my objective goals was to set up a ring-fenced buffer savings account—designed to cover any gaps between my planned retirement date and the arrival of my first pension payment.

The savings was a vital buffer in the event of delays to my pension income.

**Setting Clear Timelines With The Pension Provider**

During the formal application process for an annuity/drawdown, it is vital to:

✔ Agree on realistic timelines and milestones with your pension provider.

✔ Monitor these deadlines closely until your first pension payment is received.

**Ideally, request provider deadlines and milestones in writing in order to:**

✔ Track whether your application is proceeding smoothly.

✔ Identify if your application is falling behind schedule because of a bottleneck.

By following a shared set of timelines, milestones and deadlines with the provider, both the retiree and the pension provider can work in sync, avoiding miscommunication, misunderstanding or unplanned delays.

**Monitoring & Intervention: A Strategic Approach**

The 'Monitor and Intervention' approach can be taken one step further by applying the principle: "What you can't measure, you can't manage—and what you can't manage, you can't improve."

The key takeaway is this: by collecting relevant information throughout the annuity and drawdown application lifecycle or process, you equip yourself with the necessary information to support any interventions in the event of delays.

📌 **Possible Interventions might Include:**

✔ Elevating your application to a provider's supervising manager.

✔ Escalating your case to a senior manager or director.

✔ Filing a claim for financial compensation.

✔ Gathering evidence to support a complaint to The Pensions Ombudsman.

**Using Documentation to Strengthen Your Case**

Below, you'll find an example of the type of information that I collected during my pension income application process.

**By using the information in the table below, I was able to:**

✔ Successfully intervene in several delayed cases.

✔ Secure five figure compensation due to excessive provider delays.

Without going into too much detail here, the one recurring theme across all my claims was systemic incompetence on the part of pension providers.

**Figure 35.0 Information To Be Collected For Monitoring Intervention**

| Information | Action | Comments |
|---|---|---|
| **Milestones of key progress events related to pension application** | Note and confirm back in writing for provider comments, any milestones agreed to by both parties. | High priority information tied to when you expect your pension income to begin. |
| **Deadlines for forms, medical information, personal information** | Ensure compliance with all provider deadlines relating to the submission of vital personal information e.g. medical forms, utility bills, identities etc. | High priority information tied to the processing and progress of your pension application. Missed deadlines might delay your application. |
| **Providers Pension Admin Contact Details** | Keep the names of pension provider contacts that you | In the event of a complaint, this information is |

| | | |
|---|---|---|
| | spoke to by phone and note the dates and time of conversations. | needed to support your case. |
| **Telephone calls to providers, especially progress chasing phone calls** | Keep details (time and date) of all important telephone calls concerned with progress checking or provision of important information relating to milestones etc. | In the event of a complaint, this information is needed to support your case. |
| **Funds Transfer from one Provider A to Provider B and vice-versa** | Keep records of when funds were transferred between providers, specifically, i.e. date of transfer from a provider and date of | Traceability of your pension pot at all times is critical. Funds can go missing during transfer of funds between providers. |

| | | |
|---|---|---|
| | receipt by the receiving provider | |
| **OMO Documentation to provider(s)** | Keep records of when OMO funds were transferred between providers, specifically, i.e. date of transfer from a provider and date of receipt by the receiving provider | Traceability of your OMO pension pot at all times is crucial. Funds can go missing during transfer of funds between providers. |
| **Letter of Authority (LOA) to provider(s)** | Keep a record of the date when the LOA was completed and returned to the provider. | Traceability of LOA pension at all times is critical. Without receipt and presentation of LOA, providers might encounter delays during pot transfer |

Intervention refers to any intentional action aimed at changing a current status or situation, either to improve it or prevent it from getting worse.

However, to intervene credibly and correct a problem—such as excessive delay in a process—a person must have a yardstick against which to measure progress.

**Facilitating Intervention**

Successful intervention requires the collection of relevant information, allowing an individual to track ongoing work progress using criteria such as:

✔ Timelines of key chronological pensions application activities.

✔ Planned milestones for critical pension application processes.

✔ Lead times for critical path pension application objectives.

✔ Deadlines for submission of key information and forms.

📌 **Example:**

If you were initially told that a task would take four weeks to complete, but in reality, it took seven weeks, this is an example of a missed timeline, milestone, or lead-time deviation.

Without timely intervention, such delays could easily snowball.

### 🚨 The Financial Impact of Delays

A three-week delay in the completion of a critical path task could mean the difference between an individual receiving an annuity or drawdown income in the middle of July instead of the third week of June.

That is why an individual should undertake regular and continuous monitoring of their pension purchase application, as it enables the retiree to intervene before the situation deteriorates further.

**However, the best approach to intervention depends on:**

✔ The severity of the delay

✔ The circumstances surrounding the issue

**Effective Methods for Intervention**

Corrective or rescue interventions should ideally be recorded in writing. Although, under the right circumstances, they can also be made via telephone, provided the retiree keeps a detailed record of the intervention (e.g. time, date, details, and contact person).

Sometimes, a quick and timely phone call is all it takes to resolve an issue that isn't progressing as it should.

Although, even if intervention is done via telephone, it's advisable to confirm the details of the call in writing afterward, to ensure a shared understanding of what actions were agreed and to give the provider the opportunity to amend any incorrect information.

An individual should consider their written complaint as the equivalent of a 'Trouble Ticket' submitted to the provider for information and potentially action.

**The Importance of a Paper Trail**

Creating a paper trail for intervention incidents and issues is critical.

🚨 **Why?**

Because a retiree might need the documentation as evidence for a compensation claim—either directly from the provider or with the assistance of The Pensions Ombudsman.

**Real-Life Examples of Intervention & Compensation Claims**

Below, I have included two actual written claims based on my interventions to two pension providers who failed to meet their promised milestones.

📌 **Redacted Information:**

✔ Provider names and commercially sensitive details have been removed to comply with non-disclosure agreements.

✔ Aside from redactions, no other changes were made to featured correspondence

The following real-life compensation claims will allow you to fully understand why I've dedicated an entire chapter to effective monitoring and intervention for pension income application.

🚨 **CAUTION:** Be warned, failure to actively monitor and intervene where necessary could have lifelong financial consequences.

🚨 **Complaining to The Pensions Ombudsman: A Word of Caution:** Before proceeding with a formal complaint to The Pensions Ombudsman, be aware that the Ombudsman is rigorous about process.

🚨 **The Office Of The Ombudsman will require the following upfront:**

1️⃣ Evidence that an individual has escalated a complaint formally to the provider for internal investigation.

2️⃣ Proof that an individual has allowed the provider reasonable time to address a complaint before seeking external mediation via the Ombudsman.

These requirements further emphasize the importance of effective monitoring and intervention during annuity or drawdown process. It's very difficult if nigh impossible to make a successful compensation claim without a document trail.

Both activities, when used together, significantly increase an individual's chances of resolving disputes successfully.

**Customer Complaints *vs.* Provider Responses**

There are two notable takeaways from the correspondences featured below consisting of (a): My complaints and (b) Provider responses.

📌 **Structuring Complaints:**

✔ The complaint should be clear and structured for maximum impact.

✔ Start with the background of the issue and conclude with an impact statement and the outcome desired e.g. compensation as in my case.

🚨 **Two critical sub-sections:**

✔ Mitigation: Allows a person to propose a solution to the problem.

✔ Conclusion: Clarifies the fix or resolution sought from the provider.

**Why is this important?**

✅ Usually, an individual intervenes because the provider initially got it wrong—meaning they may not know how to resolve an issue until it's spelt out

✅ It's up to an individual to clearly define the fix sought and explain the resolution expected to the provider.

**Understanding Provider Responses**

📌 Examining responses from Provider A and Provider B

✔ I strongly recommend reading their replies carefully.

✔ Doing so will provide an insight into how pension providers operate internally.

📌 **Key learnings from their responses:**

✔ They reveal how and why pension applications can fail.

✔ They highlight areas where intervention is necessary.

🚨 Without proactive monitoring and intervention, things can easily go wrong!

**How to Strengthen a Compensation Claim**

✔ When submitting a compensation claim, ensure all t's are crossed and i's are dotted.

📌 Why? Because if a claim lacks sufficient detail, the provider can challenge and easily dismantle it, weakening the claimant's position. This is where an individual's monitoring data becomes invaluable.

✔ Progress tracking and evidence of missed dates will bolster your case.

✔ A claim should always be submitted in writing.

✔ If unable to write it yourself, seek help from a family member etc.

**Internal Dispute Resolution (IDRP) & The Ombudsman**

🚨 **If all else fails and a provider refuses compensation:**

✔ An individual should request their case be processed through the provider's Internal Dispute Resolution Procedure (IDRP). They're legally required to do so.

📌 **Why is this important?**

—

💡 Until a person has gone through IDRP, the Pensions Ombudsman won't lift its little finger to help the individual or intervene.

The first of my complaints and claim for compensation is on the next page. Immediately after that, I've included the actual provider response to mine.

The second of my complaints and claim for compensation follows the first complaint and provider response. Here's the first of the two successful compensation claims I made. Let's go!

**Figure 36.0 Letter of Intervention & Complaint to Provider "A"**

From: Yemmi Agbebi

Date: 15 August 2023 at 09:14:32 BST

To:

Subject: Fwd: FW: Application Update

15 August 2023

Pension Spending Plan:
Customer:

Subject: Transfer of [redacted] Funds to [redacted] Retirement Administration

**Without Prejudice**

Dear [redacted],

I've taken the unusual step of contacting you directly, because six months into requesting transfer of my pension fund (£[redacted]) on an Open Market Option (OMO) basis to [redacted] the [redacted] team has consistently failed to comply with multiple requests from [redacted] and [redacted] Retirement teams. I had expected to draw annuity with effect from May 1, 2023; however, here we are 6 months later, with [redacted] and [redacted] waiting for [redacted] to provide the appropriate documents. The full catalogue of poor performance and wilful incompetence by the [redacted] support team is detailed below (please see the bottom email from [redacted]).

**1.0 Acknowledgement and Issue**

Thank you for yours on 10 July 2023, which confirmed the transfer of £[redacted] to my new provider [redacted]. Unfortunately, despite over five telephone requests from me, and at least a similar number each by [redacted] Retirement Administration and [redacted], [redacted] failed to provide with the necessary Open Market Option (or OMO) information/form mandated as part of the 1975 United Kingdom Finance Act, which allows someone approaching retirement to 'shop around for options' when converting their pension pot into an annuity. Subsequently on July 21st following the transfer to , undertook "within five working days" from that date, to forward the OMO information to . However, as of COB yesterday, Monday 14 August, have not received the information, despite several requests by and .

The failure by to provide the required OMO information to , prevents from converting the transfer into annuity. This current failure is a culmination of a catalogue of errors and disregard for process by , which began when first required the transfer on my behalf in mid-March 2023. Your failure to provide appropriate OMO information was also in direct contradiction of government guidance/legislation and Act of Parliament Paragraph 3(1)(b) Schedule 28 Finance Act 2004, which applies when a qualifying pension plan member becomes entitled to their lifetime annuity.

failure to comply with provisions of the Finance Act 2004 as well as the excessively long time it took to transfer my pension to

███, has caused me serious financial distress, notably at the worst possible time given the current, high cost-of-living crisis and environment prevailing in the UK.

**2.0 Background**

I contacted ███ mid-February 2023 to discuss my annuity plan options to which I received a reply towards the end of February. Subsequently, I contacted ███ to act for me, and on March 8, after provision of the necessary information and signed authorisations, ███ Retirement Administration confirmed the processing of my annuity application was in progress. Despite several attempts by ███ to engage ███ on the strength of my signed authorization, I received numerous complaints from ███ that ███ would neither reply to their written requests nor speak to ███ over the telephone. I intervened and telephoned ███ on several occasions but all to no avail. I specifically refer to calls made on the following dates to the individuals named, which I presumed were recorded by ███. The calls are as follows: (a) June 13 (Robert), (b) June 21 (Simon), (c) June 21 (Kane), (d) July 1 (Kane). Specific requests to ███ to call ███ ███ of ███ were ignored, even though Kane promised following our second telephone conversation to contact ███, nothing happened.

The period between mid-March until July 10 when my pension fund was finally transferred, was dominated by ███ obfuscation, maladministration, disinterestedness, broken promises and unhelpfulness. The bottom line was that a request that should have been completed latest by the end of March dragged on through the sheer ███ incompetence until the transfer on July 10. However, that was not the end of the matter. As of this morning 15 August, ███ has still not received the forms promised on circa July 21 by ███.

**3.0 My Recommended Mitigations**

a) Firstly, I request immediate ███ Director intervention and escalation, to ensure ███ provides ███ with the information requested, without which my annuity cannot be triggered or begin.
b) Lastly, I strongly request the information promised by ███ to ███ otherwise I shall escalate this matter to the Financial Ombudsman.

**4.0 Impact Statement and Compensation**

(a) Although ███ Retirement Administration first submitted my transfer request to ███ mid-March 2023, failure by ███ to effect transfer of funds under OMO in a reasonable time, meant that as of today's date (15 August 2023), I have received zero annuity payments from my pension pot. are still waiting for the OMO and other information from Had dealt with my authorised transfer request in reasonable time, the receipt of my first annuity payment from would have commenced May 1.

(b) **COMPENSATION:** On the assumption that my first annuity should have been received on May 1st (6 weeks after initial request to ), I wish to make a claim for financial compensation of £ based on March quotation of £ ; covering the periods May 1st, June 1st, July 1st and August 1st, 2023. In order to alleviate the serious financial distress delay has caused me, I would appreciate it if this compensation was paid no later than August 31, 2023. After this date, I will escalate the matter to the Pensions Ombudsman and commence legal recovery of my claim.

Best regards

Yemmi Agbebi Mobile:

**Figure 37.0 Provider "A" Response To Complaint & Compensation Offer**

To: [redacted]

Dear Mr Agbebi,

I refer to the complaint you have filed under Stage I of [redacted]'s independent Internal Dispute Resolution Procedure (IDRP).

Firstly, I would like to offer you my sincere apologies that you have felt it necessary to pursue this matter under the IDRP and that satisfactory resolution could not have been previously reached with the [redacted] Administration Team ('the Team').

As arbiter for Stage I of the IDRP, I have considered your case and set out my findings, with my decision, below.

**<u>Summary of complaint</u>**

Your complaint relates to the processing of your transfer from [redacted] to [redacted], so you could purchase an annuity, which was not processed in line with your expectations. You state that you are dissatisfied with the level of service received from the Team and have requested compensation for *'loss of annuities'* of £[redacted] + 8% interest and *'serious financial distress'* of £[redacted] + 8% interest (total of £[redacted] + 8% interest).

**Considerations and decision**

I have considered all correspondence available between the Team, yourself, [redacted] and [redacted] My decision is to uphold your complaint – I set out my findings below with how I arrived at my decision.

**Service relating to the transfer of benefits (upheld)**

The completed transfer forms were received from [redacted] on 8 June 2023. Once the Team had received this form, they undertook the required due diligence before arranging the disinvestment of funds – disinvestment of your funds began on 26 June 2023 and monies were sent to [redacted] on 10 July 2023. My findings, however, have concluded that the process could have been smoother on this occasion. Upon review of the correspondence between the Team, [redacted] and yourself (between April 2023 and July 2023), it is my view that the responses from the Team during the transfer period were suboptimal, which likely impacted the time taken to complete the transfer and your annuity purchase concluding.

Once the money was transferred to [redacted] on 10 July 2023, it is noted that [redacted] requested further information from the Team on

21 July 2023, which was required to set up your annuity – I note that the Team did not respond to this request until 15 August 2023 (following a chase up e-mail from [redacted] on 14 August 2023).

I'm sorry for the level of service you have experienced, especially considering you were looking forward to a seamless transition into retirement. [redacted] expects a higher standard of service, and this feedback has been provided to the administration team to mitigate this happening in the future.

Although your benefits were transferred to [redacted] within the permitted statutory six months' timeframe, and the Team followed the correct processes and procedures once the transfer forms were received, it is my view that the process would likely have been completed sooner should responses from the Team have been to the high standards expected.

In recognition of the suboptimal service received from the Team, I would like to offer you £[redacted] in relation to 'loss of annuities' (£[redacted] plus 8% over the May to August period) and £[redacted] to reflect the distress and inconvenience you have experienced – this amounts to £[redacted] Compensation.

**Conclusions**

When members approach retirement, it is important that the Team process the request in a smooth and seamless manner. I'm sorry this did not happen on this occasion, and we are keen to recompense you appropriately to bring this matter to an end and prevent further distress.

If you would like to accept [redacted]'s offer of £[redacted] I kindly request that you complete and return the enclosed mandate and provide your bank details. This concludes your complaint under Stage I of [redacted]'s IDRP. If you are not satisfied with the decision, you will have six months from the date of this email to refer the matter to the second stage of the IDRP, which is decided by the Trustee. This is explained in the attached IDRP form.

Although escalating your complaint to the second stage of IDRP is available to you, I would welcome a short call at your convenience should you have further queries, or you are not satisfied with my response. You can contact me directly on [redacted].

You may refer your complaint or dispute to MoneyHelper at any time. In addition to providing you with advice, they may be able to assist in mediating your dispute. Money Helpers website address is www.moneyhelper.org.uk. You can also contact them on 0800 011 3797.

You can go to the Pension Ombudsman's website to gain free advice but note the second stage of the IDRP would need to be followed before this can be reviewed by the Pension Ombudsman.

The details of the Pensions Ombudsman can be found here:

https://www.pensions-ombudsman.org.uk/.

I look forward to hearing from you about the offer of £[redacted].

Kind regards,

Secretary to the [redacted] [redacted] Trustee

[redacted] [redacted]

**Figure 38.0 Letter of Intervention/Complaint to Provider "B"**

To: [redacted]

Dear Complaint Specialist,

Pension Annuity Application No: [redacted]

Customer: [redacted] [redacted] [redacted]

**WITHOUT PREJUDICE**

## 1.0 Acknowledgement

Thank you for yours of 19 June, which though appreciated focused on the post-mortem of the catalogue of errors committed by your Pensions team, rather than offering immediate, intervention solutions, to ameliorate the distressing financial position your company has put me in. This at the worst possible time a la high cost-of-living. As you're aware, "investigations" identify process failures, internal incompetencies and lessons learned etc. As commendable as these objectives are, this postmortem at my expense is scant comfort, because it wouldn't help my current financial distress in any way.

## 2.0 Background

I was introduced and handed over to [redacted] [redacted] [redacted] [redacted] by [redacted] [redacted] in March 2023. [redacted] subsequently acknowledged receipt of my application for annuity on March 31st, 2023. I mistakenly relied on your brochure's "Our Promise To You / Customer Declaration" and the promise of 4/6 weeks annuity commencement, as a credible guide to your business operations model. In the event which turned out to be grossly inaccurate. When after 10 weeks (mid-June) I'd heard NOTHING back from [redacted], I contacted [redacted] [redacted], only to be informed there were a couple of administrative queries which no one at [redacted] contacted me about. Along the way, my £[redacted] [redacted] the pension pot sent to [redacted] [redacted] ([redacted]) was subsequently returned to [redacted]. Since [redacted] transferred the funds out, the funds returned by [redacted] could not be transferred back in and it fell into an [redacted] black hole. It took two weeks and over 8 telephone calls and 6 hours on the telephone chasing to recover my [redacted]. Then, there was the case of my £[redacted] pension pot with [redacted] [redacted], half of which I learnt from [redacted] [redacted] had not been taken into account. Meanwhile, no one at [redacted] contacted or informed me of these issues which could have been resolved promptly over the phone. Perhaps it was gross administrative incompetence, or given my unusual name unconscious bias? Your internal investigation might wish to look at these two points at least.

**3.0 My Recommended Mitigations**

a) I require an immediate [redacted] Director Escalation and Intervention in my case, in order to recover lost ground and to ensure my annuity that should have started in May begins no later than August 1, 2023. b) I am in financial distress due to [redacted] failure, consequently, I require accelerated release of the tax-free lump sum element from my [redacted] [redacted] Pension Pot. This is worth circa £[redacted]. I need these funds urgently.

**4.0 Impact Statement and Compensation**

(a) failure to progress my annuity and raise queries with me in over 10 weeks, has put me in severe financial distress. Annuities from the funds I placed with on March 31st i.e. circa (i) pot ( ) (ii) pot ( ) and (iii) (£ ); have yielded zero annuity payments as of today. (b) The returned funds (that told me nothing about) lost critical investment opportunities, resulting in potential investment loss since it was returned by . (c) **COMPENSATION:** On the assumption that my first annuity should have been received on May 15 (6 weeks from March 31), I am making a financial compensation claim of £ based on March 31 quotation and broken down as follows: (i) 15-May to 30-May £ (ii) June - £ and (iii) July £ . I would appreciate it if this compensation was paid no later than July 14, 2023. After this date, I will escalate the matter to the Pensions Ombudsman and commence legal recovery of my compensation claim.

Best regards

Yemmi Agbebi

Mobile:

cc: - Retirement Income Service.

**Figure 39.0 Provider "B" Response To Complaint & Compensation Offer**

To: [redacted]

Dear Mr Agbebi

Re: Your pension annuity application [redacted]/[redacted]

Thank you for your patience while I looked into your concerns. I've now investigated your complaint fully and would like to tell you the outcome.

You told us you were unhappy about the delays and poor service you've received from us while applying for an annuity.

[redacted] [redacted] referred you to us on 13 March 2023. We called you on 29 March 2023 to go through your options. You told us you wanted to include your [redacted] pension with the application.

[redacted] were the top provider at the time, so we sent an application to you which we received back on 31 March 2023 followed by identification documents on 6 April 2023.

We sent your application to █████ █████ on 11 April 2023, after you had your customer understanding call with us that day.

Unfortunately, we didn't follow up on the progress which resulted in █████ █████ returning the funds they'd received from ███ reference █████ / █████. This only came to light when you called us on 12 June for an update.

We sent a new application to you on 14 June 2023. This included your █████ and █████ ████ funds. We were unable to include your █████ █████ pensions as they included a Guaranteed Minimum Pension which we're unable to deal with.

We received the application back from you on 23 June 2023 and sent it to █████ █████ the same day.

████ were unable to send your funds as they now had a new reference number, F█████. This was because █████ █████ had returned the original request on the first application.

On 30 June 2023 we provided █████ ████ with the new reference for the ███ funds. █████ ████ requested your funds from ████ and █████ ██ on 30 June 2023.

On 3 July 2023 █████ ████ rejected the request for the

funds referenced [redacted] as they contained uncrystallised and crystallised funds. This is something we weren't aware of. They also told us they'd requested your [redacted] [redacted] funds reference [redacted] incorrectly.

On 4 July 2023 we sent you a new application form for your [redacted] [redacted] funds reference [redacted].

We set up a new case reference [redacted]. This had to be an in-house arrangement with [redacted] [redacted] as they contained uncrystallised and crystallised funds. They set this policy up for you on 14 August 2023.

On 19 July 2023 [redacted] [redacted] requested your funds reference [redacted] correctly with you receiving tax-free cash.

On 28 July 2023 we called [redacted] [redacted] for an update, and they told us they'd used the wrong reference number when requesting your [redacted] funds. They used the old reference instead of the new one. We made them aware of the new reference on 30 June 2023. This is something you may wish to talk to them about.

On the same day [redacted] sent £[redacted] to [redacted] [redacted], a slight increase from the original value. They also paid your tax-free cash of £[redacted].

I can see we have caused delays which caused the value of your fund to drop. This means instead of receiving £ per annum you're currently receiving £. A difference of £ per annum. To put this right, I'll pay you £.

I've calculated this by using the Maximum Perceived Life Expectancy (MPLE) of a male, which is 79 years. As you were born in this comes to years £ x = £. I'll also include £ including £ Gross interest for not receiving your annuity sooner and £ including £ Gross interest for not receiving your annuity sooner.

As you could've received your tax-free cash sooner, I'll also include £. Please note we've deducted basic rate tax of £ from the interest on your tax-free cash as instructed by His Majesty Revenue and Customs (HMRC).

If you're a higher rate taxpayer, you'll need to declare this to them. If you're a non-taxpayer, you can reclaim the tax from HMRC with a tax deduction certificate. Please let me know if this is required.

To say sorry for the delays and poor service I'll also pay you £ compensation. In total I'll pay you £.

If you could let me know the bank details to send this too, I can arrange for us to pay this to you.

I hope I've answered your questions and if you need any more help, please let us know.

**Your rights**

If you're not happy with my response to your complaint, you can refer it to the Financial Ombudsman Service (FOS), free of charge. You have up to six months from the date of this letter to do this.

The FOS will only have our permission to consider your complaint after the six-month cut-off time if the delay is the result of exceptional circumstances.

Their leaflet 'your complaint and the ombudsman', explains how they work and how they may be able to help. A link to this leaflet is as follow and a hard copy can be sent to you if you'd like one: https://www.financial-ombudsman.org.uk/publications/ordering-leaflet/leaflet

**The Ombudsman contact details are as follows:**

Financial Ombudsman Service Exchange Tower,

Harbour Exchange Square, London E14 9SR

Telephone: 0800 023 4567

Website: https://www.financial-ombudsman.org.uk/

E-mail: complaint.info@financial-ombudsman.org.uk

If you'd like to talk to us about this letter or anything else, we'll be happy to help. You can call us on [REDACTED] between 9am and 8pm Monday to Friday, or email

[REDACTED].

Yours sincerely

[REDACTED] [REDACTED]

Complaints Assessor

## Chapter

## 11 The Pensions Ombudsman

Fool Me Once Shame On You. Fool Me Twice Shame On Me

### The Pensions Ombudsman Is Coming To Get You

The Pensions Ombudsman (TPO) (📞 0800 917 448) is an independent body, established by law to handle complaints and disputes related to pension schemes in the United Kingdom (UK).

TPO provides a free service, investigating matters concerning occupational and personal pensions, as well as decisions made by the Pension Protection Fund and Financial Assistance Scheme. The Ombudsman operates impartially, reviewing the facts of each case without bias.

### The Role of the Pensions Ombudsman

In practice, the Pensions Ombudsman serves as an adjudicator with legal authority.

Unlike mediation, its role extends to issuing legally binding determinations that can be enforced in court, much like a court judgment. This ensures fairness and accountability in pension administration.

Now that we've established what The Pensions Ombudsman does, let's focus on its role in complaints and disputes between consumers and pension providers, based on my personal experience.

**Profile - The Pensions Ombudsman**

The Pensions Ombudsman oversees a sector valued at around £2 trillion *(Source: Pensions and Lifetime Savings Association)* and supports tens of millions of pension holders. To put this into perspective, the UK's GDP in 2023 was £2.62 trillion *(Source: World Bank).*

Despite its vast regulatory scope, the Pensions Ombudsman maintains strict procedural standards.

It has the power to award financial compensation in pension disputes. Despite what you might have heard, the Ombudsman is not a debt collection agency—all disputes are required to follow a strict, structured process.

## Internal Dispute Resolution Procedure (IDRP)

Under the Pensions Act 1995 (PA 1995), Sections 50, 50A, and 50B, trustees are legally required to have a formal, documented complaints procedure known as the **Internal Dispute Resolution Procedure (IDRP).**

📌 **Key Requirements of IDRP:**

✔ Trustees must provide a written customer complaints procedure and notify members of whom to contact.

✔ Trustees must follow the IDRP to handle complaints fairly and transparently.

✔ IDRP must be available upon request to any pension scheme member.

📌 **Current Complaint Procedure:**

✔ A complainant must first escalate their case through the provider's IDRP Stages I and II.

✔ The provider has a minimum of 8 weeks to investigate and resolve the dispute.

✔ The maximum upper limit for resolution is 4 months.

✔ Providers must notify the complainant within 15 days of reaching a decision.

Only after these steps are completed will the Ombudsman intervene. If due process is ignored, the Ombudsman will redirect the complainant back to IDRP.

**What Happens When You File a Complaint?**

When a person complains directly to a provider—without using IDRP—the provider will handle the complaint informally, without asking you to follow IDRP.

📌 **My Experience:**

✔ When I lodged four separate complaints against different pension providers, none of the providers asked me to follow IDRP.

✔ It was the Pensions Ombudsman who informed me that I'd skipped IDRP, and I needed to follow the structured process first.

✔ Under IDRP rules, I had to give the provider at least 8 weeks to investigate my complaint.

If the provider's response was unsatisfactory, I could escalate the case to the Ombudsman.

Although, at this point, I had to wait an additional 4 weeks for the Ombudsman to process my case.

**The Real Cost of Pension Complaints**

When I calculated the cumulative provider and Ombudsman complaints lead times, it turned out that I was looking at a minimum of 3 months' delay before I could complete my pension purchase.

📌 **Real Impact:**

✔ 8 weeks waiting for the provider's investigation.

✔ 4 more weeks waiting for the Ombudsman's review.

✔ Total: 3 months without pension income!

🚨 This is why pension applicants should have a financial buffer in case of delays to their pension income application.

Unless a person has savings set aside—as I did—or have an alternative income source, financial hardship is a real possibility.

**The Pensions Ombudsman Complaint Procedure**

The Office of the Ombudsman will not intervene or entertain a complaint until the process or criteria stated below is completed.

📌 **Step-by-Step Process:**

✔ **Initial Complaint**

A person must first raise a formal complaint through IDRP with the pension provider. Providers have a minimum of 8 weeks to resolve the issue.

✔ **Application Submission**

If dissatisfied with the provider's response, an individual should submit the complaint to the Ombudsman, including supporting documents (e.g. complaint letter and provider's response).

✔ **Review Stage**

The Ombudsman examines a complaint application to determine if it falls under its jurisdiction. Additional documents may be requested at this point.

✔ **Investigation**

If accepted, the case is assigned to an Adjudicator or Resolution Specialist, who gathers information from all parties and attempts to resolve the issue.

✔ **Initial Decision**

Based on the investigation, the Ombudsman provides an initial opinion. If unresolved, parties can request a formal determination.

✔ **Final Determination**

The Ombudsman issues a legally binding decision, which can be enforced in court if necessary.

## Final Thoughts

The Pensions Ombudsman process is thorough, fair, and impartial—but it is lengthy. Nevertheless, the service is worth its weight in gold.

📌 **Key Takeaways:**

✔ Prepare for delays—complaints can take months.

✔ Follow the IDRP process first—otherwise, the Ombudsman will redirect you.

✔ Create a financial buffer before retirement to cover potential income gaps.

Understanding this process ensures pension holders know their rights, giving them confidence and preparedness when navigating pension disputes.

## IDRP - The 'Great Filter'

IDRP (Internal Dispute Resolution Procedure) serves as a critical gatekeeping mechanism, acting as a barrier for cases that do not warrant Ombudsman intervention.

### 📌 The Role of IDRP in Filtering Complaints

In my experience, neither of the two cases where I received substantial financial compensation ever reached the Ombudsman.

✔ Once IDRP is triggered, the dispute resolution process falls under the jurisdiction of the provider's Trustees—not the provider itself.

✔ This structure minimizes conflicts of interest, ensuring impartial resolution rather than allowing providers to mark their own homework or obscure administrative failures or staff misconduct.

Since trustees are legally responsible for managing pension assets, they must act in the best interests of members, following the terms of the trust.

By excluding the provider's operational staff from the formal complaint process, IDRP reduces the likelihood of providers delaying, forestalling, or acting in bad faith.

**How Pension Providers Respond to IDRP Requests**

Despite widespread administrative inefficiencies in pension buying services, most providers are not entirely resistant to reason.

Once an IDRP request is formally submitted, the provider recognizes the next step in the dispute process—should the complaint remain unresolved—is the Pensions Ombudsman.

🚨 While escalating to the Ombudsman isn't a matter of "it's the tickets for you mate" scenario, a high-profile case could result in negative press coverage, reputational or market consequences for a provider.

**IDRP: My Encounter With The Ombudsman**

📌 Correspondence from the Ombudsman (Dated 7 Dec. 2023)

✔ Before my complaint could proceed, the Ombudsman directed me to follow IDRP first.

✔ This confirms IDRP is a necessary procedural step before escalation.

📌 **The Bottom Line**

✔ Navigating IDRP is a mandatory process before reaching the Ombudsman.

✔ Escalation to the Ombudsman should always be a last resort—reserved for unresolved disputes.

Understanding IDRP's gatekeeping role ensures retirees take structured action, preventing delays and ensuring pension disputes follow transparent, regulated pathways.

**Figure 40.0 The Ombudsman Response To My Pre IDRP Complaint**

CAS-

From: Enquiries <enquiries@pensions-ombudsman.org.uk>

7 Dec 2023, 14:52

To:

Dear Yemmi Agbebi,

Thank you for your e-mail and supporting correspondence.

The Pensions Ombudsman can help with complaints about entitlement and administration relating to workplace pension schemes and personal pensions, including delays in transfers.

In the first instance, you should contact the parties you believe to be at fault, e.g. your employer, pension scheme administrator or pension provider, if you have not done so already. Most people can resolve their problem by raising a formal complaint with the parties they believe to be at fault. If you are unable to resolve your problem, then we may be able to intervene and try to resolve the matter.

However, before we can formally investigate a complaint, it is a legal requirement that you complete, or attempt to complete, the pension provider's/pension scheme's formal complaints process. In a workplace pension scheme, this is known as the Internal Dispute Resolution Procedure ("IDRP").

If you have not yet done this, you will need to write to the business of complaint and specifically ask that your complaint be considered under their formal complaints process/IDRP.

It is up to you how you set out your complaint. However, attached is a booklet, *"Complaining to the parties at fault"*, which may help you when writing to the business at fault. You should complete your complaint and send it to the employer/pension provider/pension scheme at the address given on previous e-mails/letters you have received from them.

NB: If you do not receive a response to your complaint within a reasonable period of time (usually eight weeks); or, if you receive a response sooner than eight weeks but remain unhappy, then you can make a complaint to us straight away. We will then be able to consider how best we can help you.

We operate an (informal) Early Resolution Service as well as a (formal) Adjudication service. This means that, wherever possible, we try to resolve complaints informally at an early stage by all parties agreeing to a proposed resolution. Please note that not all complaints are suitable for early resolution in which case your complaint would follow the formal Adjudication route.

In order to make a complaint to us, once you have completed or attempted the businesses complaints process/Internal Dispute Resolution Procedure ("IDRP") as outlined above, please complete and sign an application form, which you can do here: **https://www.pensions-ombudsman.org.uk/submit-complaint**

NB: When you submit your application form, please include copies of your complaint correspondence, i.e., your initial formal complaint/IDRP to the party at fault, and their final response, if applicable.

**NB:** A complaint should usually be made to the Pensions Ombudsman within three years of when you became aware, or ought to have become aware, of the problem you are complaining about. In some cases, we can deal with complaints made outside the three-year limit, e.g. if it has been delayed due to late completion of the formal complaints process or IDRP. However, we will be unable to confirm whether we can investigate your complaint until we have received your application form. This means that, for the time being, our time limits continue to run.

**Further information and next steps:**

You may find it useful to visit our website for useful guidance on our service and FAQs: https://www.pensions-ombudsman.org.uk/faqs

Please quote our case reference number, CAS-█████████, in any future correspondence with us.

Kind regards,

The Enquiries Team I 0800 917 4487

████ █████ | Contact and Support Specialist

The Pensions Ombudsman www.pensions-ombudsman.org.uk

Follow us on: Twitter | LinkedIn

**Conclusions**

I've used the Ombudsman Service twice before, and once it gets going it operates like a well-oiled, highly effective legal adjudicator and one of Britain's best regulators along with the Financial Conduct Authority. However, in order to draw from its well of excellence, you may have to jump through a few hoops that could delay the start of your retirement income.

## Chapter

## 12 Emotional Risks In Retirement

Retirement Is Like A German Sentence. The Meaning Comes At The End

### Emotional Risks - Missing Piece In Retirement Planning

On many bookshelves lined with books such as The Dilbert Principle (Scott Adams - 2020), Who Moved My Cheese (Dr. Spencer Johnson-1998) and personal finance guides, you'll find detailed frameworks on asset allocation, the magic of compound interest, tax efficiency, and withdrawal strategies. Yet nearly all these books—however sound in numbers—omit one critical variable: *emotional risk*.

I think it's fair to say retirement for many people marks a seismic shift—not just in income but in identity and purpose. A former CEO might struggle with the loss of status, a pilot whose job it was to ferry passengers safely across the Atlantic might miss a life with purpose; while a lifelong saver into a pension might equate spending with recklessness, even when their pension pot could comfortably support their lifestyle for decades.

In the context of someone who saved diligently for over 40 years, emotional risk isn't the fear of investing or market crashes. Rather, it's the subtle, human tension between financial decisions and lived experience. It's what happens when an individual, after decades of saving, is psychologically unprepared to *spend* the very wealth they so diligently accumulated over a lifetime.

The emotional risk leads to a paradox. A person with a sizable pension pot or pots, may find him or herself, living more frugally than necessary, and missing out on the very lifestyle in retirement their unwavering pension saving habit was meant to secure. Or they may overcompensate—using newfound time and access to capital to chase status symbols, hoping to mask a gnawing lack of status or purpose.

Emotional risk in retirement can also manifest in how a person deals with uncertainty: the fear of longevity, of rising care costs, of outliving their pension pot or of losing control. Some hoard cash "just in case," while others delegate financial authority to family members or professional advisers, without understanding the implications.

The reality is wealth creation doesn't end with accumulation. On the contrary, it concludes with *decumulation*—the transition from building pension wealth, to spending the accumulated assets like a pension pot (e.g. annuity or drawdown), investments built up during the working years) to pay for retirement and so forth.

This transition from earner to spender demands not just a financial plan, but an emotional one as well.

In this light, this book encourages readers to rehearse retirement emotionally through a variety of ways not just financially—for example through DIY, learning new skills or language, staying physically active, volunteering or leaving a legacy like writing the book in you as I've done.

Because when all is said and done no pension wealth can promise purpose, personal fulfilment or provide inner peace. Only a well-thought-out emotional and spiritual journey can do that.

For starters you may wish to practice mindfulness and relaxation techniques at home or alternatively, join a local group or an online community.

Who knows, you might meet new people embarking on a similar journey as yourself. What's your internal combustion engine, what's it that drives you? After all a person's inner fire or driver defines them in all seasons.

In the following sections, I've cobbled together a practical checklist to help bring the concept of emotional risk in retirement into sharper focus:

**Checklist: Preparing for the Emotional Side of Retirement**

1. **Envision Your Retirement Days ('Future History')**
   - What does a fulfilling day in retirement look like to you?
   - Who would you like to spend time with, in retirement?
   - Which activities give you meaning or spiritually uplift you?
2. **Identify Your Emotional Anchors (Passions outside of work)**
   - What's your passion?
   - What will be your purpose when you stop being a CIO, teacher, etc?
   - What makes you get up in the morning apart from work?
3. **Practice Decumulation**
   - Try small withdrawals from savings other than your pension pot and *spend them*. How does it make you feel?
   - Are you comfortable letting go of the "saver" mindset?
   - Work with a financial advisor, to create a budget and spending plan.

4. **Test Your Comfort with Flexibility**
   - Can you adapt plans if your finances, health, or relationships change?
   - If change fazes you, try practicing how to cultivate positive emotions around change.
   - Do you have emotional support to lean on if necessary?

Decumulation is the process of spending down your hard-earned retirement pot, investments and other assets. It requires a different mindset and strategies than accumulation, but it is no less important.

Consequently, the emotional aspects of retirement should not be underestimated or ignored, instead, it should be planned with the same meticulous care and attention devoted to building your pension wealth and locking down your lifetime retirement.

5. **Define Your Non-Financial Legacy**
   - Have you created a non-financial legacy with your family? For example, one of my daughters (Alexandra) gave me a blank journal which reads *"Dear Dad, From You to Me"*—A handwritten time diary crafted to capture stories from my life.

- Have you considered mentoring someone when you retire?
- Would you consider making a series of podcasts to record your wisdom, values or belief systems for your family?

**Figure 41.0 'Dear Dad From Me To You'**

**— A Journal Of A Lifetime —**

## Chapter

## 13 Lessons Learnt

Those Who Fail To Learn From The Past Are Doomed To Repeat It

### Experience Is A Great Teacher Because It Tests First

"Lessons learnt" refers to the knowledge or insights gained through experience in carrying out tasks or activities. These lessons can be positive or negative, helping individuals to identify what worked well and what did not.

**Beyond simply reflecting on past actions, lessons learnt also serve to:**

- ✔ Prevent future failures or suboptimal outcomes.
- ✔ Embrace best practices for improvement.
- ✔ Set benchmarks for defining success.

An equally important aspect of learning lessons is uncovering potential risks or hidden challenges—or as the phrase goes, "discovering where the alligators were hiding all along."

### The Importance of Learning from Experience

Conversely, failing to apply lessons learnt results in repeating past mistakes, despite clear evidence of better alternatives.

This brings to mind the famous quote attributed to Albert Einstein: *"The definition of insanity is doing the same thing over and over and expecting different results."*

This last statement was in fact a gotcha. Because contrary to popular belief, Albert Einstein never uttered that line! The phrase actually originated from author Rita Mae Brown's 1983 novel *"Sudden Death"*—so here's a prime example of how misinformation spreads. Lesson learnt?

This example is precisely how lessons learnt work—by learning from past mistakes and missteps, an individual can make better decisions in the future.

**Lessons Learnt List: Pension Savings & Retirement Transition**

The list below represents some of the most valuable pension-saving insights that I've gathered. While not exhaustive, they offer essential takeaways that may prove useful for others exploring their pension options.

For those still figuring out their best trajectory to mastering pension wealth, please consider this list as a practical informational guide.

## Lessons Learnt: Saving for a Pension

✔ **Start Early**

The sooner a person starts saving, the longer compound interest has time to work its magic.

✔ **Save Consistently**

Build a consistent and constant saving habit and stick to it.

✔ **Understand Your Pension Scheme**

Master pension basics—ignorance is no excuse for financial disadvantage.

✔ **Maximize Contributions**

Contribute as much as is affordable, especially to take advantage of employer matching contributions—it's free money!

✔ **Monitor Investment Performance**

Review pension plan's performance regularly and adjust where necessary.

✔ **Consider Tax Implications**

Don't ignore tax regulations—understand the tax benefits and consequences of pension contributions and withdrawals.

✔ **Stay Informed**

Keep up with pension regulation updates and policy changes. This is crucial.

✔ **Be Alert for Scams**

If an out of the blue pension deal sounds too good to be true, especially from cold callers, it's almost likely a scam!

✔ **Avoid Early Withdrawals**

Resist the temptation to dip into pension savings early—the longer it remains untouched, the higher the return.

✔ **Seek Professional Advice**

Consult certified and regulated financial advisers to enhance your pension approach and strategy.

Consider Pension Wise (📞0800 731 0469) and MoneyHelper (📞0800 138 7777) for free, impartial, professional guidance.

**Lessons Learnt: Income Drawdown v Annuity**

✔ Monitor Provider Performance & Keep Records

Track provider progress during annuity purchase or drawdown set-up and record all important interactions.

**✔ Intervention & IDRP Process**

If issues arise, complain promptly and trigger the Internal Dispute Resolution Procedure (IDRP) when necessary.

**✔ Understand the Difference**

Drawdown allows flexible withdrawals, while annuities provide a guaranteed lifetime income—both are taxed as income.

**✔ Assess Your Risk Tolerance**

Drawdown carries market risks and ongoing fees, whereas annuities are more secure but offer lower returns.

**✔ Consider Longevity**

Annuities protect against outliving savings, whereas drawdown depends on how carefully funds are managed.

**✔ Compare Costs**

Understand the fees involved in both options to avoid excessive erosion of savings due to management fees.

**✔ Tax Efficiency**

Evaluate the tax implications of withdrawals, especially those taken before the legally authorized pension age.

**✔ Review Regularly**

Consistently reassess your drawdown strategy to ensure you don't run out of money.

**✔ Market Performance Matters**

Drawdown is influenced by market fluctuations, while annuities remain stable.

**✔ Consider a Hybrid Approach**

A combination of drawdown and annuities may offer the best balance of security and flexibility.

## Chapter

# 14 Help With The Cost-Of-Living

Age Is An Opportunity No Less Than Youth Itself

### Financial Support For Retirees Amid The Cost-Of-Living Crisis

Pensioners, who often rely on a fixed income, face unique financial challenges compared to the rest of the population. The rising cost-of-living—particularly inflation—has made it increasingly difficult for retirees to keep up with essential expenses, including energy, food, and housing costs.

As a result, many over-65s who depend on pensions struggle to afford rising bills, leading to fuel poverty and difficulties with basic necessities. Despite these challenges, several financial support options exist to help pensioners stay afloat and maintain a reasonable quality of life. Below is a non-exhaustive list of free resources worth exploring for those on a low income.

### 1. Assistance with Benefit Claim Forms

One of the key challenges pensioners encounter when applying for benefits is completing claim forms, whether digitally or in print.

Several agencies offer assistance, particularly for pensioners with mental health conditions, disabilities, or limited access to technology.

📞 **Support Agencies:**

✔ Age UK – 0800 678 1602 (Open 8 AM–7 PM, 365 days a year)

✔ MIND – Support Line: 0300 102 1234 | Infoline: 0300 123 3393

✔ Rethink Mental Illness – 0808 801 0525

✔ Scope (Disability Support) – 0808 800 3333

✔ Extra Help Unit (Help to Claim Service) – 0800 144 8444

✔ Citizens Advice Bureau (CAB) – 0800 367-222

✔ MoneyHelper (Pension Dispute Resolution) – 0800 011 3797

✔ Disability Centres Support Workers – 0800 121 4600 | Textphone: 0800 121 4523

**2. Checking Eligibility for Benefits**

Even if you're already receiving a pension, you may be entitled to additional benefits that could significantly boost your income.

📌 **Key Benefit Options and Contact Details:**

✔ **Pension Credit – 📞 0800 99 1234**

If you're on a low income, Pension Credit can top up your weekly pension income and unlock other support, such as free TV licences for over-75s.

✔ **Attendance Allowance – 📞 0800 731 0122**

If you have a disability or health condition that affects your daily life, 'Attendance Allowance' can help cover additional costs.

✔ **Housing Benefit – 📞 0800 99 1234 | Textphone: 0800 169 0133**

If you rent your home, you may qualify for housing cost assistance.

📌 **Check Your Eligibility Online:**

🔗 https://www.gov.uk/ UK Government Portal

🔗 https://www.turn2us.org.uk/ Turn2Us Benefits Calculator

📞 **Alternatively, contact the Pension Service for Pension Credit inquiries:**

✔ **Main line:** 0800 731 0469

✔ **Textphone**: 0800 731 0464

✔ **Welsh-language:** 0800 731 0453 | Textphone: 0800 731 0456

✔ **Relay UK (for those unable to hear or speak on the phone):** 18001 then 0800 731 0469

**3. Energy Bill Support**

Rising energy prices make heating and electricity more expensive, but financial help is available:

✔ **Winter Fuel Payment**

If you were born on or before 25 September 1957, and with total annual earnings not exceeding £35,000 (tax year 2025/26), you may qualify for this annual tax-free payment to help with heating costs.

✔ **Warm Home Discount Scheme**

Check whether your energy provider offers this scheme, which provides a one-time discount on electricity bills.

✔ **Priority Services Register**

Contact your energy provider to join this free service if you are pension-age or have specific needs.

You'll receive tailored assistance, such as advance notice of power cuts.

**4. Council Tax Discounts & Rebates**

Many councils offer reduced Council Tax for pensioners, particularly if you:

✔ Live alone
✔ Have a disability
✔ Are on a low income

📌 Contact your local council to explore eligibility and apply for discounts or rebates.

**5. Food & Essentials Support**

If grocery expenses become difficult, the following community resources can help, including: Food banks, voucher schemes, community fridges, and local support groups.

✔ **Food Banks**

📞 Trussell Trust – 01722 580 180

Operates food banks across the UK, offering free food parcels to those in need.

✔ **Community Pantries**

Local initiatives providing affordable groceries at reduced prices.

📞Feed The Hungry - 0303 3000 484

✔ **Healthy Start Vouchers**

📞 0300 330 7010

If you're caring for grandchildren under four years old, you may qualify for milk, fresh produce, and vitamin assistance.

✔ **Free Food Parcel From The U.K. Government**

📞 **0800 367-222 or please contact your local Citizens Advice**

You can access a food parcel delivery if you obtain a referral from your local Citizens Advice, GP, a social worker, a school, or your local council.

Some food banks also allow you to self-refer if you can explain your situation.

**6. Free or Subsidised Travel**

Many retirees qualify for free bus travel under Concessionary Bus schemes.

**Some councils also provide:**

✔ Discounted taxi cards

✔ Senior railcards to help manage transport costs.

### 7. Seeking Financial Guidance

Managing finances during a cost-of-living crisis can feel overwhelming.

Agencies like Age UK (📞0800 678 1602) and Citizens Advice (📞0800 367-222) provide free support, including:

✔ Budgeting assistance

✔ Accessing grants

✔ Debt management strategies

✔ Energy-saving guidance

### 8. Local Support Networks

Community-led initiatives can help pensioners reduce costs while fostering social connections.

✔ Many councils and community centres operate warm spaces during colder months, allowing seniors to connect with others while saving on heating costs at home.

www.ingramcontent.com/pod-product-compliance
Lightning Source LLC
LaVergne TN
LVHW100254210926
848480LV00003B/918